# ORANGE COUNTY
## CHRONICLES

*Phil Brigandi*

THE
History
PRESS

Published by The History Press
Charleston, SC 29403
www.historypress.net

First published 2013

Manufactured in the United States

ISBN 978.1.62619.133.4

Library of Congress CIP data applied for.

# CONTENTS

# INTRODUCTION

Orange County is one of the best-known—and yet least understood—counties in America. Too often, people who try to describe and dissect our county never seem to get beyond the glitzy image created by the media of Tuscan villas by the sea with waving palms outside and beautiful people inside.

But Orange County is much more than just "the O.C." It's also the suburban neighborhoods of Orange, the barrios of Santa Ana, the townhouses of Brea, the apartments of Anaheim and the planned communities of Irvine. It's Little Saigon, Little Texas, Los Rios, La Palma, La Habra and Silverado Canyon. With a population of more than 3 million people, Orange County is a multifaceted, diverse and rapidly changing place.

One of the things missing from the many attempts to explain Orange County is an understanding of its past. Too many reporters, feature writers and even scholars don't seem to grasp that the roots of our county's identity run far deeper than the emergence of modern Orange County in the 1960s. I hope this book will help in some small way to fill that gap.

Of course, this is not a "complete" history of our county. That book will probably never be written. Instead, I have chosen to focus on a few important episodes and events that have influenced our history from the 1760s to the 1960s. These stories reflect many common themes in the history of this area including transportation, agriculture and the birth (and sometimes death) of communities. There are many, many other stories still waiting to be told.

Several of these stories have been published before in various forms (some more than once). "The Birth of Orange County" first appeared in *Orange Countiana*, the Orange County Historical Society's annual journal. "The Stearns Ranchos" and "Breaking New Ground" were previously published in the *Branding Iron*, the quarterly journal of the Los Angeles Corral of The Westerners. Others began as talks (or parts of talks) or various newspaper and magazine articles. All have been revised to a greater or lesser degree.

At its best, local history can help give all of us a sense of connection to the past, a sense of belonging and a sense of place. We are all part of a larger story.

Here are a few highlights.

# THE MARCH OF PORTOLÁ

Spain came to California with the cross and the sword. Together, Franciscan padres and Spanish soldiers worked to colonize the land and convert the Indians to Christianity. The King of Spain wanted to expand his far-flung empire. The padres sought to save souls. The cross came under the leadership of Father Junípero Serra. The sword was under the command of Captain Gaspar de Portolá. In the spring of 1769, they established the first tentative Spanish outpost in California at San Diego.

Their next goal was the bay at Monterey. While Father Serra remained in San Diego to found California's first mission, Portolá gathered up about forty of his most trail-ready soldiers and set off north into a largely unknown land. Accompanying him were Lieutenant Pedro Fages in command of a group of Catalonian soldiers; Sergeant José Francisco Ortega, who would lead the scouting party; military engineer Miguel Costansó; fifteen mission Indians from Baja California to help with livestock and supplies; and two gray-robed Franciscan Fathers: Juan Crespí and Francisco Gómez. Along with one hundred mules, the party stretched out over a quarter of a mile as it rode out from San Diego on July 14, 1769. (For many years, it was believed that José Antonio Yorba—patriarch of the famous Orange County ranchero family—was one of the Catalonian volunteers who accompanied Portolá, but his name never appears in any records of the expedition. It seems that he came in 1771 with the first group of reinforcements.)

The Portolá Expedition members were the first Spanish explorers to pass through what is now Orange County. They quite literally blazed the trail for much of the history that would follow in the next seventy-five years. Missions and ranchos grew up along their trail, and many of the place names they bestowed survive to this day.

We are fortunate that Portolá, Costansó and Crespí all kept daily journals of their trek. Father Crespí's account is by far the most valuable, but for more than two centuries, it was primarily known through an abbreviated and heavily edited text. Then, after decades of research, historian Alan Brown identified the actual "field draft" covering the march north among the archives in Mexico City. It is the actual journal carried by Crespí along the trail. In 2001, Brown published it in translation, along with Crespí's first revision of his journal, copied out soon after their return. While Portolá's route has long been known to historians, Crespí's original journal adds a wealth of new detail about the land and the people they discovered along the way.

In the early 1900s, historians began to leave their desks and libraries and set out into the field, with the diaries of early explorers in hand, to attempt to establish the routes they traveled. The routes of Anza, Lewis and Clark and others were closely studied. In Orange County, the best fieldwork on the march of Portolá was done by historian Don Meadows (1897–1994) beginning in the 1920s, when much of the area was still largely unchanged. The results of his research—first published in 1963—are followed here.

By the time the Portolá Expedition reached the edge what is now Orange County on July 22, 1769, the order of march was well established. Sergeant Ortega and a handful of soldiers rode ahead each day, scouting the trail. Portolá and the main party followed, riding on mules, with the Indian vaqueros following behind, driving the pack mules. They carried supplies for five months on the trail. Their pace seems intolerably slow, but they were not just trying to cover ground. They were seeking a practical route north, clearing brush and cutting down banks at creek crossings. It was the beginning of El Camino Real.

A notable incident took place as the party reached the edge of Orange County. As the men set up camp on a little creek, the scouts reported that in the Indian village nearby, they had noticed a little baby who seemed close to death. Fathers Crespí and Gómez both went to look for the child.

They found the little girl in her mother's arms. "We gave her to understand, as well as we could, that we did not wish to harm the child," Father Crespí wrote, "only to wash its head with water, so that if it died it would go to Heaven." The mother allowed them to approach, and Father Gómez baptized the dying child. Learning that another little girl had been badly burned in a fire, they sought her out as well, and Father Crespí baptized her, giving her the name Margarita Magdalena. Their anxious desire to baptize these little girls reflected the padres' belief that no one could enter heaven without the rites of the Holy Catholic Church. For them, saving souls was the whole purpose of the colonization of California, and these two little girls were the first to have the ancient rite performed over them. Costansó calls the spot the *Cañada del Bautismo*; today, we know it as Cristianitos Canyon, for the two little Christians.

The next day, July 23, Crespí reported, "We crossed two hollows with two creeks, dry ones, but both hollows well lined with sycamore trees and large live oaks." That is, across Prima and Segunda Deshecha Canyons in San Clemente. There was a village in one of the canyons, he added, later noting that the villages they had passed all had dogs living in them. They also passed two "mines" where the Indians extracted red and white earth "to get the [body] paints which are their normal dress." Finally, the party dropped into San Juan Canyon about four and a half miles above the present mission site. The canyon was "lined with a great deal of trees, sycamores, willows, large live oaks, cottonwoods and other kinds we could not recognize."

The men camped on the north side of the canyon, near where Gobernadora Canyon comes down. "It is a well-watered spot," Crespí noted, "one for founding a good-sized mission at."

In contrast to Crespí's wealth of details, Portolá's diary entry for the day is terse at best: "The 23rd, we proceeded for four hours. Much pasture and water, and many trees."

The next day, the party went up Gobernadora Canyon past two more villages where the Indians came out to greet them. "No telling what they were saying to us," Father Crespí noted. The Indians here (and in many other places they passed) had burned off the hillsides to encourage the growth of new plants to harvest.

The men climbed out of the canyon and across the top of Cañada Chiquita, and after about three hours, they made camp near the southern end of Trabuco Mesa. "A grand spot here, for a good-sized mission," Crespí wrote. "There is a stream in this hollow [Trabuco Creek] with the finest and purest running water we have come upon so far." Climbing the one hill on the mesa, the men could make out San Clemente and Santa Catalina Islands (which were already known by those names).

"We made camp close to a village of the most tractable and friendly heathens we have seen upon the whole way; as soon as we arrived they all came over entirely weaponless to our camp...and have stayed almost the whole day long with us." Crespí showed them his crucifix, asked them to kiss it and spoke to them about God, getting some of the children to

The ruins of the Trabuco Adobe along Trabuco Creek, circa 1930. This was an outpost of Mission San Juan Capistrano, founded in about 1806. The hills in the background look much as they did when the Portolá Expedition camped here in 1769. The area is now a part of O'Neill Regional Park. *Courtesy the First American Corporation.*

repeat *amar a Dios* (love God). "These Indians here, alone, have won my heart completely, and I would have stayed with them gladly...They have very good baskets, bowls, and a sort of rushwork-wickerweave baskets made very close-woven of rushes, and very fine."

"They came unarmed," Costansó noted, "and showed unequalled affability and gentleness. They made us gifts of their humble seeds, and we presented them with ribbons and trifles."

Unmentioned in the diaries (but documented just a few years later), during their stay on the mesa, one of the soldiers lost his blunderbuss gun—in Spanish, his *trabuco*. This was serious incident on the far frontier, and the other soldiers took to calling the area by that name. Father Crespí named the spot San Francisco Solano, as it was his Saint's Day on the Catholic calendar. But as would happen many other times, it was the soldiers' nickname that ultimately stuck.

Here on Trabuco Mesa (now the site of the city of Rancho Santa Margarita), the Portolá party laid over for a day to rest. The Indians continued to visit the camp. Father Crespí noted the many different tribal languages that they had already met on their way north. "Every day, we can plainly recognize that there is a change in the language." He jotted down a short list of words—the first ever recorded for the people the Spanish would later call the Juaneño. *Pal* meant water, *temete* meant sun, *junut* was bear, *suichi* was rabbit, *sucuat* was deer and *pat* meant antelope (in fact, he mentioned seeing six antelope the next day). All of these words are easily recognizable as examples of the Shoshonean language group.

On the afternoon of July 26, the men set out again, planning to march on into the cooler hours of the evening. They headed northwest across the head of Oso Creek, then across Aliso, Borrego and Agua Chinon Canyons. Father Crespí mentioned the grapevines they saw along the way before dropping down into valley near what would later become the El Toro Marine Corps Air Station—"a very extensive plain, of which the limit could not be discerned by the eye," said Costansó.

They halted near what is now Lambert Reservoir, expecting to make a dry camp, but Padre Gómez noticed a green spot on the hills above which proved to be a spring. The padres named it San Pantaleón. Others called it the *Aguage del Padre Gómez*. A century later, American settlers dubbed it Tomato Springs for the vines they found growing wild there.

On the Catholic calendar of Saints' Days, July 26 is St. Anne's Day, which most likely gave us the name Santa Ana. Don Meadows suggested that the mountains were named first. Alan Brown assumed that the scouts must have named the river first. But the name does not appear in any of the diaries, and the Santa Ana River would start with a more dramatic name, as we shall see.

On July 27, the party set out early, keeping to the edge of the foothills to avoid the marshy valley floor. Meadows noted that they passed between Red Hill and Lemon Heights, as the Camino Real later did, before making camp along a creek they named Santiago (St. James, the patron saint of Spain) about half a mile above Chapman Avenue.

"We made camp close to a stream," Crespí wrote, "which, while saying our prayers, Father Gómez and I have surveyed…We saw the water, wherever allowed by the great many trees, the wild grapevines, rose bushes, tule-rush, and other plants…It is a very large stream…[which] flows through the midst of this large plain of apparently very good soil." Here was a good site for a mission, he suggested. Interestingly, he also noted seeing "a stake weir, made by the heathens, at the water that we saw, by which they had it split into two large flows each taking its separate course in among the trees here." (By

Looking northwest across the hills in the Tomato Springs area on the Irvine Ranch. This photo was taken by Don Meadows in 1925 while he was tracing the route of the Portolá Expedition through Orange County. *Courtesy Special Collections, the UC Irvine Libraries.*

"heathens," of course, he simply meant that the people they met were not Catholic believers.)

The next day, the men made a short march "along the skirts of the range" to a large river, about twenty-five or thirty feet wide and a foot and a half deep. There were cottonwoods, willows, sycamores and other plants there, as well as catfish swimming by. They made camp on the southern side, just below the hill at Olive Heights, about where Orange-Olive Road now meets the Santa Ana River.

On the opposite bank was a large village (possibly *Hutuknga*, a well-known Gabrielino village in the coming years). The Indians brought them gifts of food, and their chief made a speech. Captain Portolá replied with gifts of beads and a handkerchief. "They are all very well-behaved, tractable folk, who seem somewhat lean—though the men very strongly built—and food must be in short supply with them," Crespí noted.

But the most memorable event for July 28, 1769, was a strong earthquake, followed by two aftershocks. "The first and most violent must have lasted the length of a Creed, the other two less than a Hail Mary," according to Crespí (an interesting way to estimate time, to be sure)—in other words, about a minute and perhaps twenty seconds each, respectively, Brown wrote. And so this spot was named *El Dulcisimo Nombre de Jesus, del rio de los Temblores* (the Most Sweet Name of Jesus, of the river of the Earthquakes).

"This is the most beautiful spot, with a great amount of soil and water…for founding a mission at; a spot finer than all of those behind us," Crespí wrote. The Indians, he added,

> *urged us not to go away. In order to have us remain, they pointed out for us one man who is their chief and the owner of all of this land. Our Sergeant [Ortega] and the two of us Fathers told them we would come back and when we did, would make a house for the Sergeant and for ourselves (and one for God that He might be worshipped by them), and upon our saying this, such tears of joy and happiness sprang to their chief's eyes as touched the hearts of all of us. And would they allow me to, I would most gladly return in order to stay with these poor wretches for their conversion and the good of their souls…Blessed be God, for I trust the hour is near that they shall know and worship Him.*

Even though Portolá and his men were the first Europeans to explore California by land, the Indians had already acquired a few Spanish trade items from farther east. They showed the party "nine cutlasses without hafts, along with four or five eyeless matting needles and a thick spike about half a yard in length, all of which they gave us to understand have been given them upcountry toward the north by some people there like ourselves, and we also understood there to be Fathers like ourselves," Crespí wrote. "Whether this means they have a connection with New Mexico or the Apaches we cannot tell."

The next day, the party crossed the river with difficulty (this was July, remember). Its route angled off to the northwest, west of Placentia, according to Meadows, crossing Chapman Avenue in what is now Fullerton at about Acacia Street. The men climbed the low hills northeast of Hillcrest Park and camped on top. There was an Indian village nearby along Brea Creek, above where the dam now stands.

The Spanish were courteous guests. "We learned from these heathens that the only water in this district was the little village pool, which could only serve for the people," Crespí explained, "and [so] the mounts [mules] went unwatered this evening."

On July 30, they crossed La Habra Valley, climbing the hills out of Orange County where Hacienda Boulevard does today. When they reached the river beyond, they had to build a rough bridge (in Spanish, a *puente*) to get across, giving us a whole other group of local place names.

Continuing north, the men reached Monterey Bay on September 30, 1769, but were unsure if it was the place they were seeking. Pushing on, they eventually reached the southern end of San Francisco Bay—until then, unknown to the Spanish.

With supplies running low and a known route before them, their trip back to San Diego went much quicker. Where they had spent a week in July crossing what is now Orange County, they made the return trip in just four days in January 1770, camping again on the Santa Ana River, at Tomato Springs and in San Juan Canyon.

Returning north in April 1770 to found the mission and presidio at Monterey, they met many Indians out hunting—something they had not seen on their previous visits during the summer and winter. This time, they stayed farther west after leaving the Santa Ana River, avoiding the hills on either side of La Habra Valley.

Father Crespí's constant notes on possible mission sites proved influential. Father Serra initially called for Mission San Gabriel to be placed on the south side of the *Rio Temblores* (the Santa Ana River), but the padres sent to found the mission in 1771 (apparently influenced by the soldiers) selected a different location, farther north. Still, in some early documents, the mission is called San Gabriel de los Temblores. Its records list more than 240 Indians from *Hutukgna* who were baptized there between 1773 and 1790.

Again in 1775, it was determined that another mission would be founded at or near San Francisco Solano on Trabuco Mesa. But instead, the new mission of San Juan Capistrano was founded in San Juan Canyon. Ortega was there in command of the soldiers sent out with the padres.

However, eight days after the founding Mass was celebrated, word arrived from San Diego that the Indians had risen up and attacked the fledgling mission there. All work at San Juan Capistrano stopped as the men hurried south. Almost exactly one year later, on November 1, 1776, Father Serra made a fresh start at the same location.

This was not the mission site we know today—a fact that has led to decades of controversy. The original site up the canyon didn't offer enough water for farming, so in October 1778, the mission moved downstream to its current location. Even the mission registers were changed. Originally, Father Serra noted that the canyon site was called *Quanis-savit* by the local Indians, but a later hand changed this to *Sajirit*—presumably the native name of the new site.

The memory of the move survived, even in the 1840s, when the Rancho Mission Viejo (Old Mission) was granted. The name eventually became attached to some adobe ruins at the mouth of Gobernadora Canyon, but

In the summer of 1948, a group of California horsemen re-created Portolá's march through California from San Diego to San Francisco. Here, they ride along Sixth Street in downtown Santa Ana (now Civic Center Drive). San Luis Obispo county supervisor Dick Kleck—dressed as Portolá—is riding in the center of the group. *Courtesy the Old Orange County Courthouse Museum.*

they had actually been built in the 1840s by Juan Forster, the English-born owner of the rancho. But mission scholars could find no evidence of the move, and many argued that it had never happened.

Then, in the 1960s, a cache of mission reports turned up that provided the first contemporary documentation of the move. The original site had been about two miles below Portolá's campsite, and the present mission site is about two miles below that.

So, where would that be? Once again, it was Don Meadows who unraveled the mystery. Part of the confusion, he realized, was that the Camino Real had moved along with the mission, and the original Portolá route had been abandoned. This had misled several scholars. Then he took to the field, and after studying the area, he concluded that the original site was on the south side of San Juan Canyon, on a small mesa owned by the Lacouague family then planted to citrus. They reported finding many Indian artifacts over the years, and Meadows felt sure that this was *Quanis-savit*. Today, the site would be somewhere in the gated communities near Camino Lacouague, above San Juan Creek Road.

The Rancho Mission Viejo was not the only rancho to preserve a name from the early days. Next, to the north, was the Rancho Trabuco, and the Yorba and Peralta ranch, south and east of the Santa Ana River, became known as the Rancho Santiago de Santa Ana. Finally, in the far north, the Rancho La Habra seems to recognize the pass Portolá crossed to leave the valley in 1769. In Spanish, one name for a pass is *abra*, but when it becomes *the* pass, an *H* is added to separate the two *a*'s, and thus we have La Habra.

In 1963, Don Meadows wrote, "Viewed from the perspective of almost two hundred years, the march of Portolá has glamour and romance, but for the soldiers who were making the long journey it was only a job ordered by the King of Spain. There was no glamour in the odor of sweating mules and the sting of eye-reddening dust. The romance of being the first Europeans to cross over the land was lost in the daily business of pushing ahead."

# DROUGHT, DEBT AND DEVELOPMENT

## The Story of the Stearns Ranchos

In 1860, Abel Stearns was one of the richest men in California…and one of the ugliest. In 1835, during an argument over a keg of brandy, a drunken sailor stabbed him repeatedly with a knife, leaving him disfigured in face and speech. Behind his back, his Mexican neighbors called him *Caro del Caballo* (Horseface). Yet he married one of the most beautiful girls in California and made her very, very rich.

Born in Massachusetts in 1798 and orphaned by age twelve, Abel Stearns went to sea as a boy. He traveled the oceans on trading ships, first as a sailor and later as a supercargo or agent, responsible for buying and selling hides, tallow and manufactured goods. In 1822, he began trading in Mexico, and in 1826, he moved to Mexico City, where he became a naturalized citizen two years later.

He came to California in 1829, when the missions still dominated the area. He soon settled in Los Angeles, where he opened a store and continued to deal in hides and tallow. He often served as a middleman between the trading ships on the coast and the ranchos of the interior. In 1834, he established a warehouse and store above the harbor at San Pedro, where he dominated the Los Angeles trade for the next decade.

In 1841, Abel Stearns married Arcadia Bandini, the daughter of a prominent ranchero. She was fourteen; he was forty-three. It was by all accounts a happy marriage, although childless. Instead, Don Abel raised cattle.

Photographs of Abel Stearns are rare. Perhaps he was embarrassed by his appearance. Here he is in his later years. *Courtesy the First American Corporation.*

# A YANKEE RANCHERO

Cattle were the backbone of the California economy in the first half of the nineteenth century. Their beef fed the population, and their hides and tallow were sold and traded for manufactured goods shipped in from the United States, England, Mexico, South America and Asia.

Before 1834, the missions owned most of the cattle in California and controlled much of the grazing land. The only *rancheros* were a few retired Spanish soldiers who had decided to stay on in the new land.

Under Spanish law, all of California was considered the property of the king. The missions were given the right to use their share on behalf of the Indians, but they did not own the land. The handful of *pueblos* and *presidios* scattered along the coast were given four-square leagues each (about eighteen thousand acres), some of which was held in common and some divided among the settlers.

But what of the retired soldiers and their growing herds? In 1784, Governor Pedro Fages took it upon himself to allow a few of them to start their own ranchos outside the mission and pueblo lands. These were not land grants, but rather concessions or grazing permits—a right to occupy the land that still belonged to *El Rey*.

One of the first three lucky recipients was Manuel Nieto, who was given the rights to use all the land between the Old San Gabriel River (now the Rio Hondo) and the Santa Ana River, from the foothills to the sea. Later, after protests from the missionaries at San Gabriel, the northern end of the Nieto concession was cut off, leaving him a miserly 163,000 acres.

In 1821, Mexico broke away from Spain, taking California with it. In 1828, a new law was passed giving the government the right to grant up to eleven square leagues (some forty-eight thousand acres) to any Mexican citizen of good standing who would develop and stock the land. The impact of the law was delayed in California until 1834, however, when the secularization of the missions began, stripping them of their lands and authority.

It was also in 1834 that Manuel Nieto's heirs petitioned the governor of California to formally grant them the land their family had controlled for half a century. Faced with the size of the Nieto concession—and the number of descendants—Governor José Figueroa made five separate land grants to various members of the family: Santa Gertrudes, Los Coyotes, Las Bolsas, Los Alamitos and Los Cerritos. Suspiciously soon afterward, Governor Figueroa was able to purchase the Rancho Los Alamitos for a nominal fee.

It was the Rancho Los Alamitos that first caught Abel Stearns's eye. After considering the purchase for several years, he bought the twenty-eight-thousand-acre grant in 1842 and began his new career as a California ranchero.

While the hide and tallow trade was the basis for the California economy in the 1830s and '40s, there were two main drawbacks. First, there just wasn't much money in it—that is, not much cold, hard cash. It was largely a matter of trade and barter. And that was the second problem. The manufactured goods the rancheros needed had to be shipped in from great distances, at great expense.

The Mexican-American War of 1846–48 and the Treaty of Guadalupe Hidalgo, which ended the war and transferred California from Mexico to the United States, did little to change the hide and tallow trade. But just days before the treaty was signed, a carpenter looked down into the millrace of a new lumber mill and spotted a few yellow flakes. James Marshall had found gold at Sutter's Mill, and California would never be the same.

Beginning in 1848, tens of thousands of miners flooded into Northern California. The surge in population was so great that California skipped being a territory and jumped straight to statehood in 1850.

Los Angeles County (which included the future Orange County) was a long way from the gold fields, but the rancheros down here felt the impact of the Gold Rush in their own way. Cattle that were once worth perhaps four dollars for their hide and tallow were suddenly selling for as much as seventy-five dollars on the hoof for beef to feed the hungry miners. Men like Abel Stearns grew wealthy on Northern California's gold.

And not a moment too soon. For with American statehood came newfangled American ideas like property taxes, which weighed heavily on the families who measured their land in thousands of acres.

Worse yet, while the United States had pledged to recognize all existing property rights in California as part of the Treaty of Guadalupe Hidalgo, pressure from Northern California, where a growing population was hungry for land, led Congress to pass the Land Act of 1851, which treated all California land titles as suspect and required the owners to prove their claim before it would be recognized by the U.S. government. That meant government commissions, hearings, testimony, attorneys, judges and courts, and all the expense that went with them. Some ranchos were not confirmed for decades.

It is common to speak of the old Hispanic *Californios* struggling to adapt to the new American laws of taxes and land commissions (along with high interest rates on loans). But in fact, the race of the ranchero made little difference under this new system. Foreigners had been moving to California for decades. A few, like Stearns, had become Mexican citizens and secured land grants of their own. Except perhaps for the language barrier, they faced the same challenges as the Californios—and often with the same results.

To make matters worse, in the mid-1850s the Gold Rush began winding down. The population in the gold fields dropped, and so did the demand for beef, driving prices down. To stay afloat, the rancheros began borrowing money. The interest rates were staggering—3, 5, even 10 percent, compounded monthly.

At first, this rising tide of debt worked to Abel Stearns's advantage. As a merchant as well as a ranchero, he had easier access to hard cash, which he was willing to lend at prevailing rates. If the rancheros paid off the note, good; if they could not, better. The debt would allow Stearns to sue them, receive a judgment and extract payment—sometimes in livestock, other times in land.

The Ranchos of Los Coyotes and La Habra were both owned by Italian-born Juan B. Leandry when he died in 1843. Andrés Pico then arranged to buy a half-interest in the ranchos from Leandry's mother, borrowing $6,000 from Abel Stearns to close the deal. In 1851, when he couldn't pay the money back, Don Abel claimed Pico's half. Leandry's widow, Francesca, married Francisco O'Campo. They also borrowed money from Stearns. He foreclosed on them in 1860, and Los Coyotes and La Habra were his.

The Rancho Las Bolsas was granted to Catarina Nieto in 1834. Seven years later, she allowed her brother, Joaquin Ruiz, to carve out the Rancho Bolsa Chica as a separate grant. In 1849, Señora Nieto sold a half-interest in the Bolsas to Ramon Yorba and his siblings. Yorba's wife was a Morillo, a niece of José Justo Morillo, who was married to Catarina Nieto's daughter, Maria Cleofa, giving him an additional claim on the Bolsas as well. In time, the Morillos also borrowed money from Abel Stearns, and Ramon Yorba borrowed money from John Downey and James McFarland, who were using the same debt and foreclosure method to build their ranching empire. Don Abel bought Yorba's note from them, and either bought or loaned and foreclosed on the interests of his siblings. With all the pieces in place, Abel Stearns forced the sale of the Ranchos Las Bolsas and Bolsa Chica at public auction in 1861, and he bought them both.

Other ranchos were purchased outright. Juan Pacifico Ontiveros sold 1,165 acres of his Rancho San Juan Cajón de Santa Ana to the original Anaheim colonists in 1857. He gave another 3,900 acres to two of his sons. The remaining 21,000 acres, *mas ó menos*, he sold to Abel Stearns in

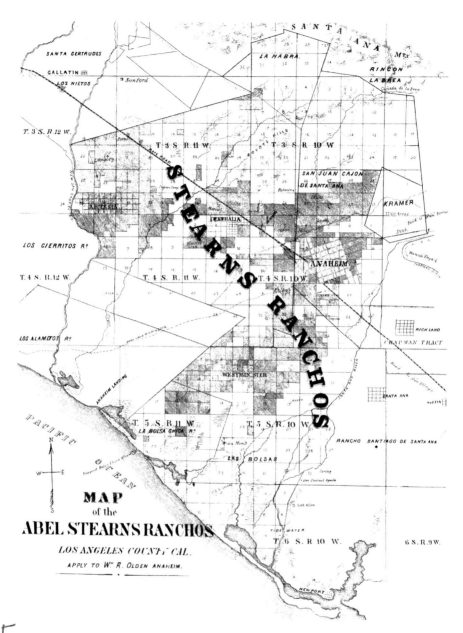

The Stearns Ranchos covered much of western Orange County and southeastern Los Angeles County, along with parts of what is now Riverside County. This map was issued in about 1873 to lure settlers to the area. *Courtesy the First American Corporation.*

1863. Stearns eventually controlled some 200,000 acres in Los Angeles and San Bernardino Counties, "the largest land-and-cattle empire in southern California," according to historian Robert Glass Cleland.

But while Stearns was busy foreclosing on others, his own debts were mounting. He had begun borrowing at the same usurious rates, and as his cattle ranges expanded, so did his operating expenses and property taxes.

The final blow for Stearns, along with many of his contemporaries, came in 1863–64, when a withering drought swept Southern California, decimating the open range. Cattle died by the thousands for lack of food and water. As Don Abel's income dried up, his debts mounted and his taxes went unpaid. He was forced to borrow more and more just to hold on to what he had.

He was not always successful. In 1865, financier Michael Reese turned the tables on Stearns, forcing the sale of the Rancho Los Alamitos—his first and favorite rancho—to settle a $20,000 debt. Mired in debt now, Stearns borrowed money anywhere he could, offering ranch land as collateral to secure his debts again and again. His ready cash was gone. His income was almost nil.

# A Matter of Trust

There seemed to be no good way out for Abel Stearns at this point. He had forced the sale of so many other ranchos for debt, but now his own end was in sight. But land would always have value, and there were people who could see that. At the last moment, Abel Stearns was rescued. In a remarkable real estate deal, his debts vanished, and he was set back on the road to wealth.

Alfred Robinson was one of Abel Stearns's oldest friends. He had first come to California on a trading ship in the same year as Stearns. The two had done business together many times. Now Robinson looked at his old friend's situation and at his many ranchos. In those vast acres, Robinson saw an opportunity. The land was good for more than cattle ranching. Subdivided and properly marketed, it could be sold off in small parcels to farmers and town builders.

So, Alfred Robinson rounded up a group of San Francisco investors to buy and market Stearns's land. The men who agreed to put up the cash were Edward F. Northam, Charles B. Polhemus, Edward Martin and Sam

Brannan. Robinson would manage the operation and get a share of all sales. Together they formed the Robinson Trust. Then they made Abel Stearns a very generous offer. In return for almost all of his Los Angeles and San Bernardino county lands, they would pay him $50,000 up front to settle his debts, give him a one-eighth interest in the trust and pay him $1.50 per acre out of every future land sale.

Don Abel knew a good thing when he saw it. On May 25, 1868, he deeded more than 177,796 acres of choice Southern California real estate to the Robinson Trust. Much of the land was in what is now Orange County, including the Rancho La Habra, the Rancho Los Coyotes, a portion of the Rancho San Juan Cajón de Santa Ana, the Rancho Las Bolsas and the adjoining Bolsa Chica—that is, most everything west of the Santa Ana River (except the Rancho Los Alamitos) north to La Habra.

Northam, Polhemus and Martin had all come to California during the Gold Rush and gotten rich in mining, railroads and real estate. Sam Brannan had come a few years earlier, with a group of Mormon colonists, but had left the church and became involved with all sorts of real estate schemes. Edward Northam had the largest share at three-eighths, and Edward Martin had another quarter. Charles Polhemus got an eighth, as did Abel Stearns. Sam Brannan also got an eighth but quickly sold it to George Howard and A.V. Bowman, giving them each a sixteenth share.

To sell their new holdings, the Robinson Trust organized the Los Angeles & San Bernardino Land Company. The name was a little unwieldy, so most everybody just called it the Land Company or, more simply, the Stearns Ranchos.

The land was subdivided on the usual government pattern of 640-acre sections. The square sections were then divided up into farm lots ranging from 20 to 160 acres. Sales began almost immediately, and within just a few months, more than 12,000 acres had been sold.

During its first few years, the Los Angeles & San Bernardino Land Company launched an aggressive marketing campaign in California, across the United States and even into Europe. Brochures, maps and advertisements were everywhere. The Land Company also hired agents to represent it and handle sales in San Francisco, Los Angeles and Anaheim.

Charles B. Polhemus's cousin, Henry D. Polhemus, was the company's representative in Anaheim for the first few years. He was followed by William R. Olden, a consummate booster. Later, Robert J. Northam, a nephew of Edward Northam, took over. "Diamond Bob" would cut quite a figure locally for a number of years.

But the Robinson Trust had a problem, and his name was Abel Stearns. Despite having signed away almost all of his property, Stearns continued to act as if he still owned it. He was still grazing cattle and horses on the land. He made offers to sell portions of the ranchos at prices different from the Land Company rates. And worst of all, he rented large swaths of land for sheep grazing. In 1870, Stearns rented out portions of the Ranchos La Habra, Los Coyotes, San Juan Cajón de Santa Ana and Las Bolsas to various sheep ranchers at about ten cents per per head for the season.

All of this was quite improper since Stearns no longer controlled the ranchos. Plus, the sheep, as his new business partners pointedly reminded him, ate the grasslands right down to the roots, leaving the area barren— and harder to sell. Even Alfred Robinson finally grew disgusted with his longtime friend.

The problem was solved in 1871 when Abel Stearns died, once again a rich man. His widow, Arcadia Bandini de Stearns (later Mrs. Robert S. Baker), survived him by forty-one years and was one of the richest women in Southern California when she died in 1912.

# New Towns

The sale of the Stearns Ranchos led to the founding of a number of new communities in the 1870s; some of them survived and thrived, while others faded and failed.

The area around Anaheim filled in quickly with new farms. By 1870, enough families had settled southwest of town to support their own school district, which they dubbed Fairview. But the community never even grew large enough to have its own post office, and the school district was annexed to Anaheim in 1888.

North of Anaheim, the local ranchers voted to form their own school district in 1873. There was already talk of a separate Orange County then, which may be why they chose the name Orangethorpe (*thorpe* is an Old English word for village). Orangethorpe barely ever rose to the level of a town, yet it was briefly its own city (1921–23). The school district survived until 1954, when its territory was divided between Anaheim and Fullerton.

Reverend Lemuel P. Webber, the new pastor of the First Presbyterian Church of Anaheim, saw an opportunity in the vast Stearns Ranchos. In

West Center Street (now Lincoln Avenue) in downtown Anaheim, circa 1873. The area around the townsite settled up quickly once the Stearns Ranchos went on sale. *Courtesy the Anaheim Public Library.*

1870, he arranged to take control of some seven thousand acres of the Rancho Las Bolsas to found a Presbyterian temperance colony he called Westminster. He laid out a townsite, and no one could buy land there without his approval.

To advertise his new town, Reverend Webber published an extensive "Prospectus," which explained:

> *It has long been a cherished purpose of the projector of this colony, to establish a settlement of persons whose religious faith, notions of morals and education, should be so nearly alike, that they might cordially co-operate from the first, in the maintenance of a Christian Church and a superior school…*
>
> *The members of this colony, although not strictly required to be members of any church, yet shall be such as can conscientiously and heartily unite with the other colonists in encouraging and supporting the sanctuary service to be established at an early day by the Presbyterian Church. It is not intended or desired that any one's religious views shall be interfered with or constrained. Yet only those who freely and from principle can endorse this*

*requirement, and can feel at home with the Presbyterian Church are invited to cast their lot with us.*

The land was divided into eighty farm lots of 40, 80 or 160 acres, originally priced at thirteen dollars per acre. The land sold well; within four years, almost the entire tract had been sold, and the Robinson Trust agreed to set aside another 3,000 acres for prospective colonists.

But the town itself was slow to develop. A schoolhouse was built in 1872, and a post office was opened in 1874, along with the first store, a Grange cooperative. Water for the tract came largely from artesian wells. The water table was high enough then that water would rise naturally to the surface from wells drilled down some seventy-five to two hundred feet.

It was not until 1872 that Reverend Webber organized the First Presbyterian Church of Westminster, with seventeen charter members. But Westminster was never truly a Presbyterian colony. While Reverend Webber expected settlers to be sympathetic to his denomination, he was unwilling to force his faith on anyone, and by 1876, a Methodist church had been established on the townsite. It was joined two years later by a Congregational church, and both these congregations completed their own sanctuaries before the Presbyterians' church was dedicated in June 1879.

Reverend Webber did not live to see any of these first three churches built. His efforts to build up Westminster were cut short by tuberculosis. He died on September 25, 1874, at the age of forty-two.

By the late '70s, Westminster's growth had slowed to a crawl. Ivana Bollman, who wrote her master's thesis on the colony, suggested several possible reasons, including the lack of good transportation facilities, the early death of Reverend Webber, problems with alkali soil and the many marshy areas that needed drainage, not irrigation. It was not until the 1890s that large-scale drainage projects began in the area, opening up more and more land for farming.

As the population grew in the area between Westminster and Anaheim, another new town emerged. Garden Grove was the brainchild of Alonzo G. Cook, who arrived in 1874 and bought 160 acres from the Stearns Ranchos. When a school district was formed to serve the area about one year later, it was Cook who suggested the name Garden Grove. One old pioneer recalled:

*Some objected, thought it not appropriate as there was nothing that could be called a tree in the whole district, but Mr. Cook said, "We'll make it appropriate by planting trees and making it beautiful."*

In 1876, Cook began selling off portions of his property to other settlers, and the community of Garden Grove was born. He provided a lot for the school and helped to organize a local Methodist church. He was a partner in the first store in Garden Grove, and the first postmaster (1877) was his father-in-law.

In order to capitalize on the colony idea, the Los Angeles & San Bernardino Land Company laid out several tracts, hoping to lure a town founder and a group of ready-made settlers. Its first tract was known as Savanna, in the Buena Park/La Mirada area. In 1869, the Land Company filed a tract map and began boosting Savanna in its sales literature. But the tract never took off. Historian James Guinn's description of his first visit there later that year has been quoted many times:

*In 1868 and '69 Southern California was in a transition state. The era of cattle and sheep raising as distinctive industries was on the decline. Grain and fruit-raising were beginning to be recognized as the coming industries of that region. Los Angeles was experiencing its first real estate boom. Every steamer was crowded with immigrants seeking cheap lands for homes. The Stearns ranchos in the southeast part of the county, comprising over two hundred thousand acres, had been subdivided into small tracts and thrown on to the market at prices varying from $2.50 to $10 per acre. Just before we cast loose from the wharf at San Francisco an active young man came aboard the steamer with an armful of boom literature, the first I had seen. It was maps, plots and circulars descriptive of the lands of the Los Angeles and San Bernardino Land Company (the Stearns ranchos). These he distributed where he thought they would do the most good. A map and description of the city of Savana [sic] fell to my lot. The city was described as located on a gently sloping mesa overlooking the valley of the Santa Ana. Sites had been reserved by its founders for churches and schools, and a central location was held in reserve for a city hall. A few weeks after my arrival I visited the city. I found it on the western slope of the Coyote Hills, about six miles north of Anaheim. Long rows of white stakes marked the line of its streets. A solitary coyote on a round-top knoll, possibly the site of the prospective city hall, gazed despondently down the street upon the debris of a deserted sheep camp. The other inhabitants of the city of Savana [sic] had not arrived, nor have they to this day put in an appearance.*

In 1875, the Land Company decided to give it another try. The Southern Pacific railroad to Anaheim had just been completed, and on the south side of

The E.B. Foster home, with its young fruit trees, was typical of many of the early ranches in Orange County. The failed townsite of Centralia was located in the Buena Park area. *History of Los Angeles County, 1880.*

Coyote Creek, at what is now the Orange County line, a station was established known as Costa. The Land Company proceeded to lay out a 480-acre tract around Costa station. It was laid out for farming, with the smallest lots still two acres each. There was no defined townsite. The tract was dubbed Centralia, "from its proximity to the center of the valley"—five and a half miles from Anaheim, six miles from Artesia and six miles from Westminster.

Perhaps learning from Savanna's failure, the Land Company never filed a tract map with the county. A number of settlers bought land in the tract, and in 1876, they formed their own school district. But as late as 1880, the Land Company was still looking for a town founder to lure colonists to the area. The local papers speculated that the price was just too high—sixty dollars per acre—for anyone to make a profit. Much of the area later became part of Buena Park.

In the end, most of the Stearns Ranchos were sold to individuals on a contract basis, with an initial down payment and three years to pay. The buyers also had to pay 10 percent interest on the unpaid balance, as well as any and all taxes due on the land. Once all the money had been paid, a deed was issued, signed by Alfred Robinson as trustee.

The deeds wisely reserved to the company land for future roads, along with "the use and control of cienegas and natural streams of water, if any, naturally upon or flowing across, into, or by said granted tract." In other words, the Land Company retained all the water rights. In arid Southern California, that was a significant clause. But in fact, it was little used. The general complaint was that the company didn't do enough to develop the water resources on its lands, especially during the dry years of the 1870s.

After an initial sales surge, things slowed down for the Los Angeles & San Bernardino Land Company in the mid-1870s. Along with drought conditions, it also faced some failed marketing schemes and an invasion of "squatters."

## SQUATTERS

The squatter problem stemmed from the Santa Ana River, which had been used as a boundary for several of the early ranchos. In the floods of 1825, the river shifted several miles southeast to drain into Newport Bay. That meant—according to some—that the land between the two channels was not part of any rancho and thus was public land, open for homesteading.

It seems that some of the squatters actually started out as buyers, signing sales contracts with the Los Angeles & San Bernardino Land Company then later deciding to stop making payments, taking their chances as the battle wound its way through the courts. Most of the squatters (or "settlers," as they preferred to be called) took up land on the east side of the Rancho Las Bolsas. Before long, they began forming their own communities.

Nathan Sears and a group of his kin settled east of Westminster in what would be the Little Saigon area today. The *Anaheim Gazette* usually referred to the area as the Sears Settlement, but in 1871, when the settlers organized a school district, they named it Bolsa Grande.

The Bolsa Grande School was the Sears Settlement's only civic asset. Although references to the settlement continue on into the 1880s, there never seems to have been any "town" there—no post office, no store, not even a blacksmith shop.

Other squatters settled southeast of Garden Grove in an area that became known as the Willows. Horace Head, who came to the area with his family as a boy in 1876, later recalled, "In the early days the land for a mile or more adjoining the river was a jungle of willows, cottonwoods and sycamores, with an occasional patch of cactus or tules. It was occupied by rabbits, quail, coyotes, wildcats and squatters." The Willows never even grew to the status of settlement, although for a few years the Garden Grove School District maintained a second schoolhouse there.

To the south, in 1879, another group of settlers formed its own school district, which it called New Hope. South of Westminster, the Ocean View School District was formed in 1875. Nearby was the similarly named Bay View District.

But the heart of "Squatterdom" was Fountain Valley. The name celebrates the artesian wells, which flowed like fountains without pump or windmill over much of the lowlands. There were enough settlers in the area by 1875 that the Los Angeles County Board of Supervisors created the Fountain Valley Township, giving them a constable and a justice of the peace. A year later, a school district and a voting precinct were established. There were even hopes of a post office, but it never materialized.

The squatter question affected everyone in the area. The Stearns Ranchos, of course, wanted ownership of the land they had purchased. They also faced the challenge of selling land in the disputed area. Who wants to buy a lawsuit? This uncertainty slowed the growth of the area, which meant less business for the surrounding towns.

The squatters, on the other hand, were risking years of work and improvements to their homes and farms and still faced years of struggle in court if they ever hoped to prove their case.

As long as the final government patents to the Ranchos Las Bolsas and Santiago de Santa Ana were not complete, the uncertainty remained. In 1872, the Stearns Ranchos ordered all the squatters off the Bolsas. Instead, more and more kept coming. By the beginning of 1876, the *Anaheim Gazette* reported that there were more than two hundred squatters and their families living on the Bolsas, supporting four public schools.

In 1877, the federal government at long last recognized all the lands between the old and new beds of the Santa Ana River as part of the Rancho Las Bolsas. The location of the river at the time of Nieto's 1784 concession did not enter into it, it ruled, since the government patent was based on the 1834 grant of the Bolsas, when the river was already in its current position.

The Newport Methodist Episcopal Church South (right) is the best surviving landmark of Gospel Swamp, east of the Santa Ana River, which served squatters and settlers alike. Built in 1877, it is shown here in 1911. The little church still stands at the northeast corner of MacArthur and Greenville in south Santa Ana, where it is now part of the Greenville Country Church campus. *Courtesy the First American Corporation.*

Yet more squatters continued to arrive, settling on other parts of the Bolsas, even north of Westminster, far from the disputed lands. In May 1878, the Land Company finally decided that it had had enough. It was time to evict the squatters. But in a neat trick, the company did not sue the squatters directly. It leased a portion of the rancho to a man named Edwin P. Whitmore, who was said to be from New York. This allowed the case to be filed in the U.S. Circuit Court in San Francisco rather than the Los Angeles County Superior Court, adding to the trouble and expense for the squatters. More than three hundred of them were named as defendants in the suit of *Whitmore v. Asbill et al.*, which sought their removal and $50,000 in damages.

Through various legal maneuverings and postponements, it was not until July 1879 that the circuit court heard the case. The entire hearing lasted only about four days. With the Bolsas now patented all the way to the river, the squatters tried a new argument. The Rancho Santiago de Santa Ana had not yet been patented, and wasn't its western boundary the river as it flowed in 1810? That meant the Bolsa squatters weren't on the Rancho Las Bolsas at all, but on the Santiago, which overlapped with the Bolsas. Shouldn't both claims be thrown out and the land opened for homesteading?

But the judge would have none of it. He ruled that the Bolsas patent was binding, and finding no questions of fact to be decided, he instructed the jury to find for the plaintiffs. The Stearns Ranchos came out on top.

In October 1879, eviction notices were served on all the squatters. All agreed to leave peacefully. "Many who are able to do so will purchase" their farms, the *Anaheim Gazette* reported, but the majority could not afford the Land Company's prices. They took with them everything they could carry. Some even picked up their houses and moved them into Westminster or other nearby communities. Others moved farther afield. Quite a few went to San Diego County and settled in the area around Julian and Warners Ranch. Forty families moved up to Buell's rancho in San Luis Obispo County, where the town of Buellton was later born.

The last of the squatters to go was a Frenchwoman and her children, who had been too ill to move when the others "were given the grand bounce" and was allowed to remain until June 1881. By then, the population across the lowlands had dropped precipitously.

By 1880, the Ocean View and Bay View School Districts were both left with fewer than thirty school-age children and were unable to receive any more county funds. Ocean View managed to survive, but the Bay View District was abandoned and merged with Fountain Valley in 1886. The

Looking west on Fourth Street, in Santa Ana, circa 1878. The tall trees on the left mark the crossing of Main Street. *Courtesy the First American Corporation.*

Fountain Valley voting precinct, which had registered 89 voters in 1876, cast only 26 votes in the presidential election of 1880. The federal census that year found only 143 residents in the entire township—the smallest population in what is now Orange County.

A cloud still hung over the disputed lands until the patent to the Rancho Santiago de Santa Ana was finally issued in 1883. And even then, the controversy continued. But where the newspapers had originally supported the squatters against the evil Land Company, by the 1880s, most came to believe that the endless battles did more harm than good and were holding back the development of the whole region.

The last of the lawsuits was finally settled in 1889, when Justice Field of U.S. Supreme Court ruled against the Bolsa squatters. Once again, the company gave the few remaining squatters a chance to buy their land and time to harvest their crops before moving out.

# A REORGANIZATION

Over the years, the owners of the Robinson Trust continued to change as the stockholders bought and sold, or died and others inherited their interest. By the late 1880s, Charles Polhemus was the only one of the original investors still active with the trust.

Squabbles between the various owners hampered the Land Company's efforts in the 1880s, and for much of the real estate "boom" of 1886–88, the Stearns Ranchos were not even on the market.

An attempt was made to reorganize the trust in 1886, but for some reason, it fell apart. Finally, in August 1887, the owners incorporated as the Stearns Ranchos Company, with headquarters in San Francisco and a capital stock of $92,160, divided into 9,216 shares. Charles B. Polhemus, Moses Hopkins, Eleanor Martin and William H. Howard were all on the board of directors, along with James B. Randell, attorney John T. Doyle and Charles A. Grow, who would serve as secretary of the corporation for many years.

"Diamond Bob" Northam stayed with the company through all these twists and turns. Besides serving as its agent in Anaheim, he was a partner in one of the downtown stores and served as mayor of the city in 1885–86.

But in 1893, Northam's management of the Stearns Ranchos' interests was called into question by Charles Polhemus and his son, George. They claimed that Northam had been skimming cash from land sales and leases and had pocketed $15,000 from the sale of sheep manure, which had been sold for fertilizer. Northam replied that by his accounting, he was actually owed money from sales commissions, and he added that he had assumed the sheep manure belonged to the sheep ranchers whose flocks had produced it on lands they leased from the company.

The attacks against Northam seem to be another symptom of the continuing conflicts between the various stockholders. Northam claimed that George Polhemus had always been a "bitter enemy" of his uncle, while the Hopkins heirs and Charles Grow stood solidly behind Northam, who hurried to San Francisco to present his side of the story.

The San Francisco papers devoted a great deal of space to the charges, even before they were formally presented to the Stearns Ranchos Board of Directors. Someone—apparently from the Polhemus side—had leaked a draft of the investigation to the press. The *San Francisco Chronicle* reported that "Northam, so the report as it now stands will charge, devoted too much of his time to recreation and pleasure to properly attend to his land interests, and consequently many good opportunities of a business nature were allowed to slip by."

Northam's admittedly flashy lifestyle not withstanding, the financial questions seem to be more about his accounting practices than any actual embezzlement. And with the Hopkins estate owning 72 percent of the stock—and the fact that the company was still paying regular dividends—the matter was soon settled.

Northam soon retired to a 1,600-acre ranch on the Bolsa Chica where he grew barley, walnuts and apricots and ran cattle and horses. In 1901, he sold out to a group of investors that formed the West Coast Land & Water Company, which founded a new community along the coast there. The investors called their town Pacific City, but the original company was soon bought out, and the town was renamed Huntington Beach.

Northam moved up to Los Angeles that same year, and three months after his first wife died, he married a woman thirty-three years his junior. A decade later, they were just about ready to divorce when Northam fell ill, and his young wife decided to stay with him to the end. He died in 1912.

Sales of the Stearns Ranchos continued in the late nineteenth and early twentieth centuries, but not at the old pace. As late as 1893, the company still owned about eighty thousand acres, worth an estimated $3 million. That value increased as oil was found in the northern Orange County foothills in the 1890s. In some cases, the land was leased rather than sold to the oil companies, providing another source of income for the stockholders.

The Robinson Trust's first three recorded sales in 1868 were all in what is now Orange County. The last land sold in Orange County by the Stearns Ranchos seems to have been 9.44 acres along Magnolia Avenue, west of Anaheim, in 1926.

The company was dissolved by decree of the San Francisco Superior Court in February 1927 and the assets divided among the remaining shareholders. After almost six decades, the Stearns Ranchos Company faded into history.

# THE BIRTH OF ORANGE COUNTY

On June 4, 1889, the residents of the southern end of Los Angeles County went to the polls and voted to form their own county. It was the culmination of two decades of struggles, setbacks and political maneuvering on all sides.

"Historians, generally speaking, are not partial to failures," wrote James M. Guinn, the first historian of the long drive to create the new county. Yet the twenty years of failure and frustration that preceded the birth of Orange County set the stage for everything that happened in 1889. All of the same issues, many of the same methods and even some of the same players weave their way through all these earlier attempts.

When the new state of California was first divided into counties in 1850, what is now Orange County was simply the southern end of Los Angeles County. Over the next six decades, hardly a session of the state legislature went by without bills introduced to divide, merge or realign our counties, taking California from its original twenty-seven counties to fifty-eight today.

Except for the founding of Anaheim in 1857, the southern end of Los Angeles County saw little settlement until 1868, when the Stearns Ranchos north of the Santa Ana River went on sale and the old Rancho Santiago de Santa Ana to the south was partitioned. Over the next few years, half a dozen new towns were born, the population surged and the drive to create a new county began.

Anaheim was at the forefront of the earliest county division efforts, under the leadership of the always energetic Max Strobel. In the winter

Anaheim mayor Max Strobel was the leader of the earliest county division drives. *Courtesy the Anaheim Public Library.*

of 1869–70, he began drumming up support for both the incorporation of the city of Anaheim and the creation of Anaheim County.

The German-born Strobel was later described by James Guinn as

> [a] *soldier of fortune and a Machiavel in politics, he was always on the losing side. A man of versatile genius and varied resources, a lawyer, an*

*editor, an engineer, an accomplished linguist and a man of education, his exchequer was always in a state of collapse and the brightest efforts of his genius were wasted in staving off his creditors.*

Under California's original constitution, the state legislature controlled both city incorporation and county formation, so it was off to Sacramento that Max Strobel went in January 1870, armed with a batch of petitions and a war chest donated by local residents to fund his lobbying efforts.

Strobel's proposed Anaheim County was much larger than today's Orange County. It took in all of Los Angeles County below the Old San Gabriel River (the Rio Hondo), extending much farther to the north and east. Long Beach, Downey, Norwalk, Whittier, La Puente, Covina, Azusa and Pomona (only Downey then existed) would all have been part of Anaheim County.

Strobel's key arguments would be repeated again and again over the next twenty years: it was inconvenient to go all the way to Los Angeles to transact official business; the roads were bad, and the county had not seen fit to build any bridges in the south; and the City of Los Angeles monopolized most of the county offices, making it a veritable case of taxation without representation.

The *Los Angeles Star* (the principal paper in the county at the time) opposed the split, citing the county's relatively small population and the threat of higher taxes for all. For support, Strobel turned to some of the largest landowners in the southern end of the county, including Juan Forster, William Workman, Juan Temple, Billy Rubottom and Benjamin Dreyfus.

A bill incorporating the city of Anaheim was soon secured, and Strobel would go on to be elected the city's first mayor. The Anaheim County bill passed the California Assembly but faced growing opposition as it moved on to the Senate.

Los Angeles County assemblyman M.F. Coronel fought back from the start, saying—no doubt correctly—that a majority of his constituents opposed the split and that "it would be a step of unmitigated and inexcusable folly." Higher taxes, he said, would surely result. "The proposed measure would only be profitable to a few landed proprietors at Anaheim, and a class of idlers, who hope to earn an easy subsistence by filling the newly created county offices." As for distance to Los Angeles, it was only thirty-six miles from Anaheim; some other parts of the county were as much as seventy-five miles away!

The Senate Committee on Counties and County Boundaries returned the bill without recommendation, citing the costs of a new county government, which would be a greater burden on the residents than "the inconveniences to which they have become accustomed" (that is, their long, uncomfortable trips to the county seat). Perhaps, the committee suggested, it would be better to wait until after the voters had the chance to express their opinion at the polls, rather than merely by petitions and letters.

To fight the growing opposition, Strobel wrote home for more money. According to Guinn, some folks said that Strobel had been spending too much money on high living during his stay in the state capital ("fighting the tiger," as Guinn slyly put it), but others sent fresh contributions.

There is an old, old story (even Guinn only repeats it as a rumor) that the night before the Anaheim County bill came to a vote in the Senate, Strobel gave a "champagne supper," hoping to drink some of his opponents under the table so they would miss the morning's vote. Instead, it was Strobel who succumbed to the libations, and the bill failed.

But Strobel was not deterred. The state legislature would not meet again until 1872, giving him plenty of time to drum up more support. In the summer of 1871, he announced a new campaign for county division and his own campaign for a seat in the Assembly so he could push through the split.

To promote his dual goals, Strobel launched his own newspaper, the *People's Advocate*. However, said Guinn, it only "succeeded in dividing the divisionists into two factions—the Strobel and the anti-Strobel."

Anaheim's original newspaper, the *Anaheim Gazette*, was among the anti-Strobel crowd, although it was still solidly for division. On June 24, 1871, the *Gazette* published a call for a county division convention over the signatures of a number of prominent local residents. Strobel was not among them.

Other communities had been founded in the Santa Ana Valley since the winter of 1869–70, and their leaders joined Anaheim in the call for county division. William H. Spurgeon, the founder of Santa Ana; Columbus Tustin, who founded the town that bears his name; and Abram L. Bush, a big investor in Santa Ana real estate, all signed the call for a division meeting.

But the plan went awry when only three communities held elections to select delegates to the convention. Strobel's plans were also thwarted when he lost his bid for election that fall. The *People's Advocate* was absorbed by the *Gazette* a few weeks later, which changed its name to the *Southern Californian* for a few years to try to expand its status. Strobel died in England in 1873 while in the midst of his final quixotic quest: to sell Catalina Island.

But once again, the division movement survived. In November 1871, a new call went out for a county division meeting in Gallatin (an all but forgotten little community that today is a part of Downey). The *Anaheim Gazette* was glad to see that the meeting was not just an Anaheim affair, so it would not "be regarded as advanced solely for the aggrandizement of our own town." Instead, it would benefit the entire area that would be "segregated from a fossilized old machine like Los Angeles County that is run by men who evidently have no interests in common with us."

The proposed county took in less territory than the 1870 bill, drawing the northern boundary at the San Bernardino baseline (about the route of the 210 freeway today). Anaheim would be the county seat, but only for the first year or two, until an election could be held. The new campaign also adopted a new name for the new county: Orange County.

Let it be said once again that Orange County was not named for all the orange groves that covered the land. In fact, there was not a single orange grove in what is now Orange County in 1871—just a few specimen trees and some nursery stock. Instead, the name played on Southern California's reputation as a "semi-tropical" paradise where lush fruits would flourish.

Petitions were gathered during the winter of 1871–72, fundraising began and a representative was selected to carry the case to Sacramento. But the bill never reached the legislature. The Southern Pacific railroad was then demanding a public subsidy equal to 5 percent of the assessed valuation of the county before it would lay tracks to Los Angeles County. "[T]hey knew that if the county was segregated their subsidy scheme would miscarry," the *Anaheim Gazette* explained a decade later. "They defeated division, secured the subsidy, and every year since, and for many years to come, the people have paid and will continue to pay interest on that enormous subsidy."

But even the power of the SP could not deter the divisionists. In 1873, they returned to Max Strobel's strategy, hoping to elect an assemblyman who would support their cause in Sacramento. The move was billed as nonpartisan. Abram Bush of Santa Ana gave up his seat on the Los Angeles County Board of Supervisors to make the run as an independent, and historian James Guinn (who was then teaching school in Anaheim) ran on the People's Reform Ticket. That seems to have split the pro-division vote, and both men lost in the elections that fall.

So, a new petition was prepared for the legislature of 1874. This time, Judge W.C. Wiseman of Anaheim offered to personally carry an Orange County bill to Sacramento and stay on to lobby for its passage. For support, he looked to legislators from Northern California, who had no qualms about dividing Los Angeles County.

Anaheim's *Southern Californian*, of course, supported the split, noting that after five years, everyone had already heard all the arguments pro and con.

The Los Angeles papers just as predictably opposed it, saying that it was only favored by a minority of county residents. "[I]t is always a minority which desires to divide," the *Californian* responded. "A majority controls and does not secede."

Most of the energy behind the bill came from Anaheim, where hopes ran high. The *Los Angeles Express* complained that "at the southern end of the county a reign of terror exists...which violently represses all expressions of our friends against the suicidal act." The *Southern Californian* claimed that it knew of only four opponents of the bill and accused Los Angeles interests of paying off local residents to write letters in opposition to Sacramento.

Judge Wiseman stayed in Sacramento for more than a month and remained upbeat right to the end. The Assembly bill died in committee in March, but Dr. Noble Martin of Placer County obliged by reintroducing the Orange County measure in the Senate. William R. Olden, local agent for the Los Angeles & San Bernardino Land Company (the Stearns Ranchos) came north from Anaheim to join in the lobbying efforts, but Dr. Martin's bill also failed.

It would be another two years until the legislature met again, so it was not until December 1875 that the Anaheimers once again began circulating petitions and looking for support in other communities. They had little luck.

Santa Ana was growing rapidly by then and had grown to resent Anaheim's dominance. So this time, William Spurgeon, Columbus Tustin, James McFadden and other civic leaders south of the Santa Ana River turned against the plan and opposed county division. To try to lure them back, Anaheim proposed a new name, Santa Ana County. But it didn't work. Santa Ana wanted the county seat, not just a name on a map.

To make sure that their new bill wouldn't get lost on its way to Sacramento, the Anaheimers put pressure on Los Angeles County assemblyman Fred Lambourne through his longtime employer, William Workman, whose twenty-four-thousand-acre ranch in the La Puente area was on the edge of the proposed county. Workman was a partner in the Anaheim Landing shipping operation and knew many of the divisionists personally. Lambourne agreed to introduce the bill "by request," presumably to give him some cover with his Los Angeles constituents.

In January 1876, the *Anaheim Gazette* (having resumed its original name) asked and answered a series of questions about the measure. County division was necessary, it said, as the only way to get out from under the rule of Los Angeles. What's more, it was inevitable, so why not now? The county debt would only grow, and public improvements would continue to be built elsewhere.

# A BILL

## TO CREATE THE

# County of Santa Ana.

## A Bill to Create the County of Santa Ana, to establish the Boundaries thereof, and to provide for its Organization.

SECTION 1. There shall be formed out of the Southeast part of Los Angeles County a new county, to be called Santa Ana.

SECTION 2. The boundaries of Santa Ana County shall be as follows: Beginning at a point in the Pacific Ocean three (3) miles Southwest of the center of the mouth of the New San Gabriel River, proceeding up said river in a North by Easterly direction to its point of divergence from Old San Gabriel River, thence in an Easterly direction along the ridge of the Puente Range until it intercepts the boundary line between San Bernardino and Los Angeles Counties, thence along said boundary line Southeasterly until it intersects the boundary line of San Diego County, thence along said boundary line Southeasterly until it reaches the Pacific Coast, thence in the same direction to a point three miles in said Pacific Ocean, thence in a Northwesterly line parallel to said coast, to point of beginning.

SECTION 3. The seat of Justice shall temporarily be at the town of Anaheim, until finally located as further provided in this Act.

SECTION 4. The Governor of this State shall, when this Act takes ef-

The bill to create Santa Ana County in 1876 was actually sponsored by Anaheim interests and found few supporters in its namesake city. *Courtesy the California State Archives.*

Was Anaheim only pushing division to get the county seat? That argument cut both ways, it replied (neatly avoiding the question), deeming it "folly" to oppose county division only on those grounds.

James Guinn took it a step further, writing an eight-page pamphlet of *Facts and Figures for the Opponents of County Division*, published by the *Gazette* to help its opponents see the error of their ways.

The Los Angeles papers, of course, enjoyed the struggle between the two sides of the Santa Ana River. The *Los Angeles Star* claimed that there was only a small group of prospective office holders and their allies behind the movement. "Really, the only reason for the new agitation arises from the fact that Anaheim knows that when the proper time comes for the division of the county, if, indeed, such a time shall arrive, Santa Ana will become the county seat."

It was in 1876 that the first suggestion was made to move the county line down to Coyote Creek, where it would eventually be placed. Instead, it was moved down to the San Gabriel River, with the northern line drawn along the top of the Puente Hills, not far from the current boundary.

Division meetings were held in Orange and Santa Ana, where speakers on both sides rehashed the usual arguments. Some of the Anaheim delegates grew testy before the meetings were through. D.W.C. Dimock of Orange summed up the opposition when he said that while he supported division, he "had no confidence in the politicians of Anaheim, as politicians were the same the world over."

William Olden remained a prominent figure on the Anaheim side, leading some to worry that the Stearns Ranchos were only pushing division because they expected to have more influence in the new, smaller county.

Anaheim sent its lobbyist to Sacramento armed with petitions. Hundreds of opponents signed remonstrances, stating their objections. But the bill never came to a vote. In the end, "[j]ealousies and bickerings, local prejudices and local ambitions defeated the measure," James Guinn groused.

Then came a five-year dry spell—literally and figuratively—as forces outside local control diverted attention away from county division. The drought of 1876–77 started the two sides of the Santa Ana River on an eight-year legal battle over water rights. And the battles over the new state constitution in 1878–79 postponed many political movements.

It was not until the state legislature prepared to meet in 1881 that county division rose again. This time, the measure found a new champion in attorney Victor Montgomery, who maintained offices in both Anaheim and Santa Ana. He even succeeded in discovering a new argument in favor of county division: the southern end of the county provided few criminals, he claimed, but still had to help pay for the busy courts and jail in Los Angeles.

On the other side, the Los Angeles papers attempted to defuse the oldest argument for division by pointing out that with the Southern Pacific railroad now running as far south as Santa Ana, a trip to the county seat was easier than ever.

The Montgomery bill followed the same boundaries as the 1876 measure. It also sidestepped the county seat question by leaving the matter up to local

The new Orange County Jail, 1897. Four years later, the county courthouse was built beside it. The jail was torn down in 1926, but its outline is preserved in the parking lot behind the Old Courthouse. The black cook on the far left of the steps was actually one of the inmates, Alexander Toppin. *Courtesy Special Collections, Cal State Fullerton Library.*

voters once the new county was approved. The name Orange County was retained. "[T]he name of the new county," Montgomery said, "emblazoned upon the map of our State, would, in my opinion, have more effect in drawing the tide of emigrants to this section than all the pamphlets, agents and other endeavors which have hitherto proved so futile."

Anaheim and Santa Ana both appointed lobbyists to carry their petitions to Sacramento. Benjamin Dreyfus, a leader in the local wine industry, represented Anaheim, while businessman and developer James McFadden served Santa Ana. Later, when Dreyfus asked to be replaced, James Guinn was sent north in his place.

This was Anaheim's last big push for county division. To fuel its efforts, the *Anaheim Gazette* devoted almost its entire front page to the division cause on January 29, 1881, and sent extra copies of the paper to Sacramento. The paper noted:

> *This county division agitation has its impulse from higher motives than mere office-seeking. It proceeds from a long-felt and deep-rooted conviction that the southern part of the county would be more prosperous if given a distinctive name and accorded its proper place at the head of the semi-tropical counties*

*of Southern California. The…county is too large, to unwieldy, too diverse in interests to be legislated for and managed by one set of officials.*

"The people of Los Angeles have themselves to blame for this movement," Anaheim attorney Theodore Lynill added. "They have habitually worked against us, especially in trying to turn emigrants away from our section. We want no more of Los Angeles county. Can you tell me why we should not have our rights under our Constitution and go our way?"

Assemblyman J.F. Crank of Pasadena was willing to introduce the bill, but the real question remained: how do you create a new county under the new state constitution? "The trouble appears to be that the ten lawyers who compose the Assembly Judiciary Committee hold ten different opinions as to the constitutionality of every bill that is brought before them," the *Gazette* complained. The committee noted that the Orange County bill was special legislation, which was specifically prohibited under the new constitution. But it also held any general bill would be unconstitutional, so counties would have to be created by special legislation. So which was it? The problem would dog every future effort at county division.

Faced with these constitutional questions, the 1881 bill was eventually withdrawn, and effort was made to pass a general county division bill that would outline the process under the new state constitution. But that measure failed to pass.

Unable to have things its way, by 1882 Anaheim had swung into the anti-division column. J.F. Crank was now running for state Senate and was said to support county division. For Assembly, Santa Ana was backing Garden Grove Democrat Dr. Henry W. Head. Questioned by the *Gazette*, Dr. Head denied that he was being run as a division candidate but reserved the right to support or oppose any petition or bill sent to him if he was elected. Armed with that equivocal promise, the *Gazette* gave him its support, and Anaheim voters helped him to carry the day.

Then, to their disgust, Dr. Head turned around and reintroduced the Montgomery bill, with one important alteration: the county line was moved down to Coyote Creek (where it is today). This excluded Norwalk, Artesia and Los Nietos, where there was active opposition to division. It also placed Santa Ana near the center of the proposed county. The bill still left the creation of the new county to the legislature, with local residents only voting on a county seat and the various county officials.

The *Anaheim Gazette* could hardly come up with enough venom to spew at Dr. Head, filling its columns with spite (sometimes in a mock Biblical style). William

Rented rooms in the Congdon Block at 302 East Fourth Street in Santa Ana served as Orange County's first courthouse from 1889 to 1901. Shown here in about 1889, the building was torn down in 1973. *Courtesy the Orange County Archives.*

Spurgeon, James McFadden and Victor Montgomery were also targets of their wrath. The fact that Dr. Head also supported Sunday Laws, which closed saloons one day a week, and "local option," where communities could vote to ban liquor entirely, does not seem to have done anything for his popularity in Anaheim.

As opposition grew, there was talk of amending the bill to allow a public vote on division—something the *Gazette* claimed was clearly unconstitutional. A general county division bill was also proposed, allowing areas with a population of more than five thousand to vote on division, but requiring a two-thirds vote for approval. A "foolish" move, noted the *Los Angeles Herald*, which opposed the Head bill as well. In the end, however, Dr. Head's bill was deemed unconstitutional by the Judiciary Committee and was withdrawn.

The county division drive in the 1885 legislature came from an unlikely source. Charles F. McGlashan, the assemblyman from Truckee (best known for his 1879 book *History of the Donner Party*), introduced a new general bill on county division in the hopes of getting past the difficulties of the new state constitution. When the bill ran into opposition, he decided to try a different approach and get just one new county created to establish a precedent—the one he chose was Orange County.

The McGlashan bill was based on the 1883 Head/Montgomery bill but added a requirement that two-thirds of the voters in the new county had to approve the split. It again placed the boundary line at Coyote Creek, so Anaheim responded as it always did in that case and opposed it. Santa Ana, just as predictably, got behind the measure through its new assemblyman, Eugene E. Edwards. Meanwhile, Los Angeles turned to its sometimes contentious assemblyman, H.T. Hazard, to marshal the opposition.

The bill survived its committee hearing and was approved by the full Assembly in late February. "The fact that it has even reached its present stage is due more to the popularity of Colonel Edwards as an individual member," the *Los Angeles Times* was forced to admit, "aided by an antipathy on the part of a large majority of the members to the member from Los Angeles city"—that is, Assemblyman Hazard.

But without those personalities in play, the bill stalled in the Senate and never got out of committee. Once again, Orange County would have to wait.

County division was again an issue in the elections of 1886. Colonel Edwards had decided to leave the Assembly and run for state Senate against Louis J. Rose of San Gabriel. Both candidates tried to position themselves carefully on county division. Edwards soft-pedaled his support for the issue, while Rose—at least while campaigning in Santa Ana—said that he would not oppose division (if the people desired it, of course).

In the end, Edwards lost, but William H. Spurgeon captured his old seat in the Assembly. Curiously, though, he made no move to introduce a county division bill during his term.

At the end of 1888, the score now stood at seven division attempts, six bills introduced, two successful votes in the California Assembly and a continuing failure to get the job done. But that didn't stop supporters of the new county from trying again.

Having failed to win a seat in the state Senate, Colonel Edwards decided to make another run for Assembly in 1888 and was re-elected. Even the *Los Angeles Times* praised him as "extremely industrious and efficient…a man of affairs, quick, nervous, energetic and a 'pusher.'"

On the Senate side, J.E. McComas of Pomona ran on the Republican ticket and pledged himself to work for county division. Besides not being from Los Angeles, he had hopes of getting a new county for his end of the county, so helping to get Orange County created would set a nice precedent.

In early December 1888, Colonel Edwards proposed yet another Orange County bill, while McComas sponsored a companion measure in the Senate.

Once again, the northern boundary was placed at Coyote Creek, and once again the *Anaheim Gazette* was livid:

> *If the bill had for its purpose the establishing of the county seat in Santa Ana, Mr. Edwards could not have arranged the boundary line with more effect. Less than one-fourth of the present county is segregated by this ridiculous dividing line…*[T]*he Coyote Creek division line smells too palpably of a Santa Ana job.*

The new editors of the *Gazette*, Charles and Henry Kuchel, went even further a few weeks later. "If Santa Ana desires to divide so passionately let her draw the dividing line to the south of us." But they took comfort in their belief that Los Angeles would ultimately defeat the measure, as it had so many times before.

William Spurgeon and James McFadden led the lobbying effort in Sacramento on behalf of the new county, while Anaheim and Los Angeles sent their own lobbyists to oppose it. There were no new issues in the arguments over county division in 1889. It was still too far to Los Angeles, too many offices were still filled by Angelenos, too few county improvements had been built in the south and supporters were just as confident the new county could be run more economically as opponents were sure it could not.

Edwards's bill originally called for the state legislature to form the new county, but he later agreed to amend it to allow for a two-thirds approval by the voters of the new county. The *Los Angeles Times* called the idea "absurd" and argued that all the voters from the whole county being divided should have a say. "[T]his is too much like cutting a man's arm off without asking his consent," it cried. If minority of the voters could vote to separate, where would it all end? (Later changes in the law would require a full county vote—thus California has not seen a new county created since 1907, when Imperial County was formed.)

The Edwards bill passed easily in the Assembly, sixty-four to six. Even Assemblyman J.M. Damron of Los Angeles voted in favor. The measure faced a tougher battle in the state Senate, but supporters were able to secure the support of enough Los Angeles businessmen to help sway the votes of some of the legislators.

Then there was the question of money. Charges of bribery had been floating around all winter. "It is an open secret that money has been used at Sacramento to carry the division bill through the Legislature," the *Los Angeles Times* announced in March, adding that six members of the "San Francisco delegation" had asked for $300 each to switch their votes to no.

If so, the *Orange News* retorted, why didn't the opponents offer to pay them off? And why would divisionists have spent the money if the Bay area representatives already planned to vote in their favor?

There is no doubt that plenty of money was sent north to aid the lobbying efforts of Spurgeon, McFadden and the other pro-divisionists, but how much of it was used to simply bribe elected officials remains unclear. At the time (and for many years after), local supporters always denied any malfeasance. But in 1926, longtime Santa Ana businessman George Edgar was asked if he remembered the battles of forty years before. "Hell yes," he replied. "We bought this county from the State Legislature for ten thousand dollars, and I went out and raised the money myself in two hours and it was a rainy morning at that."

Sam Armor, one of Orange County's first supervisors, later wrote, "There are sometimes a few members of the legislature who are looking for 'Col. Mazuma' to come to the help or hindrance of much-desired legislation. Because the rich county of Los Angeles would not distribute a large defense fund among such members, they turned against that county."

"Then, too," Armor added, "San Francisco had begun to recognize in Los Angeles a possible rival, and was glad of the opportunity to deprive her of some of her territory."

Regional rivalries and personal relations clearly played a role in the bill's passage as well. Even the *Los Angeles Times* admitted that Northern Californian representatives were likely to vote in favor of division in order to lessen the Angel City's growing importance. There was also said to be a falling out that winter between San Francisco political boss Chris Buckley and state Senator Stephen M. White, the leader of the Los Angeles delegation. James McFadden's many business connections in the Bay area also seem to have been helpful.

Santa Ana pioneer Linn Shaw later recalled:

> *"Blind Boss Buckley" swung nearly his whole flock of "lambs" into the same line-up—not for boodle, but on the request of a personal friend to whom he was under many obligations, and to satisfy a resentment on the part of many of his cohorts because the rich county of Los Angeles had not been forthcoming with the plunder which they had expected.*

The Edwards bill was approved by the Senate on March 8, 1889, by a vote of 28 to 8. After signing it, Governor Robert Waterman appointed a five-man commission to conduct the required two-thirds vote election, which was set for June 4. The war of words between Anaheim and Santa

The Orange County Courthouse, 1904. The distinctive metal cupola was removed after the 1933 Long Beach Earthquake. *Author's collection.*

Ana continued right up to the last moment, but the final outcome was never really in doubt. The official tally was 2,509 votes in favor of county division and an even 500 against. Ten precincts voted 100 percent in favor of division, and three more had only 1 or 2 votes cast against it. Buena Park voted solid against the split; Anaheim voted 231 to 12 against, and Fullerton polled 96 to 15 to remain part of Los Angeles County.

Six weeks later, voters returned to the polls to select the first slate of county officers and to finally settle the old question of which city would become the county seat. Since Anaheim's opposition had put it out of the running, Santa Ana's only real rival was Orange. But again, it was no contest. Santa Ana collected 2,504 votes for county seat to just 775 for Orange. (The best summary of the local battles of 1889 is found in Jim Sleeper's 1973 book *Turn the Rascals Out! The Life and Times of Dan M. Baker, Orange County's Fighting Editor.*)

The new county offices opened for business on August 1, 1889, and the board of supervisors held its first meeting four days later. The County of Los Angeles would mount several legal challenges to the division, but all of them were eventually turned down by the courts.

Orange County was on its way.

# CHINESE PIONEERS IN EARLY ORANGE COUNTY

Asian immigrants have long been a part of the Orange County scene. While Vietnamese and Korean immigrants are more prominent today, and the Japanese have a long history here, our first Asian pioneers came from China.

Chinese immigrants were valuable members of the local labor force in the late nineteenth century, and while the prejudice they faced was sometimes severe, their foreign way of life was a source of endless fascination for local residents. Several local communities had their own little "Chinatowns," and few were without at least one Chinese laundry or vegetable peddler.

The permanent Chinese population here was never very large—perhaps a few hundred at most—but it could grow rapidly when harvest time came around or when big construction projects were underway. In 1887, the Santa Fe had a force of 1,500 Chinese workers building its first rail lines here. Chinese immigrants also worked on many of the local irrigation projects, as farmhands and as domestic servants. Others established laundries, kept stores, grew and sold vegetables door to door or harvested abalone. Some of the businessmen also served as labor contractors, supplying workmen for various jobs. There were also at least two Chinese doctors who practiced here in the early days.

Chinese field hands were important to the celery industry that grew up in the western part of the county in the 1890s, but not everyone welcomed their arrival. Historian Fern Hill Coleman noted that around 1892,

Chinese workmen spray walnut trees on the Irvine Ranch to protect them from disease, circa 1900. *Courtesy Special Collections, Cal State Fullerton Library.*

*the anti-Chinese feeling was at a high pitch in that year and settlers resented the importation of Chinese into the district. The Chinese were threatened, their shacks burned and their tools stolen. Finally the Earl Fruit Company buildings were burned and the company employed a guard with orders to shoot anyone caught annoying the Chinese…The Orientals provided themselves with huge savage watch dogs which they chained at the doors of their shacks and for years afterwards these dogs could be seen at Chinese shacks in the celery district.*

After 1900, Japanese immigrants replaced the Chinese in celery fields, but soon the fertility of the soil began to decline and many growers switched to sugar beets.

Racial prejudice was not unique to Orange County. As early as the 1870s, anti-Chinese sentiments played a prominent role in California politics, but despite occasional acts of violence, the movement never seems to have gained much traction here.

Others sought a different path. The Presbyterian churches in both Anaheim and Orange arranged Chinese-language services and Sunday School classes in the 1870s and '80s. In Orange, night classes were also offered to teach English to the local immigrants.

Beginning in the 1860s, Anaheim was the first local community with a sizeable Chinese population and became home to the county's largest Chinatown. Eventually located just west of Anaheim Boulevard along Chartres Street (where Lincoln Avenue crosses today), the community survived on into the 1930s.

Santa Ana's Chinatown was also in the heart of downtown, at Third and Bush, with a few other stores around the corner on Main Street. Orange's little Chinatown was originally downtown, but in the 1890s, it moved to the Gardner Ranch, just outside the city limits on South Glassell Street, across from what is now Hart Park.

Orange's Chinatown was small but typical. There was a store, a laundry or two and a bunkhouse where most of the men lived. Out back, chickens wandered around the fenced drying yard for the laundry. Hung Kee ran the laundry for more than twenty years and employed a number of the other residents. Sing Lee had the last laundry there, from 1912 until the buildings were condemned in 1924.

The 1900 census found just 136 permanent Chinese residents in Orange County (54 of them in Anaheim). By 1910, that number had dropped to about 85; by 1920, there were just 26. And it was an aging population as

The last residence in Anaheim's Chinatown along West Chartres Street, circa 1935. By then, the community had all but faded away. *Courtesy the Anaheim Public Library.*

well. Congress had cut off almost all immigration from China in 1882 and denied citizenship to those immigrants already here.

It was also largely a male population, with few women and children. Many of the men had left their families behind in China when they came to California to find work. That made them especially fond of the local American children who sometimes came to visit their shops and fields. Alan LaMont, who grew up across the street from Anaheim's Chinatown in the 1920s, loved to recall the warm relationship he and his family had with their Asian neighbors. Several of the men particularly doted on his older brother, Victor, and their father knew that his son was perfectly safe when he sometimes joined them on their rounds selling vegetables. And each year, around the Fourth of July, LaMont noticed that his pennies always bought a few more firecrackers in the Chinese store than the boys who seldom set foot in Chinatown the rest of the year.

But there were problems as well. "Predominantly a community of men (initially by choice, then later by American immigration laws prohibiting the entry of women), it was not unusual for the Chinese to get into fights

This sketch of Ong Q. Tow in his military uniform was part of newspaper feature story that ran nationwide in 1898. *Courtesy Jim Sleeper.*

over gambling, property or debts where hatchets, knives and pistols were often quickly drawn and sometimes to quickly used," according to Dr. Patricia Lin in her study of Orange County's Chinese pioneers.

Some of the troubles were between men of different "companies" (immigrants from particular parts of China who had banded together for mutual support). By 1876, there were already four different companies in Anaheim. The companies often tried to settle problems between themselves without turning to the American courts. When Orange laundryman Hung Kee was attacked by members of another company in 1898, the case seemed open-and-shut. But by the time it got to trial, Hung Kee refused to testify, and the charges were dropped.

Hung Kee was one of a number of well-known Chinese merchants here. Ong Q. Tow was perhaps the best known. He was a businessman and an American citizen and even went off to war.

Tow—familiarly known as Jimmy Craig—was born in Sonoma County in about 1870 and educated in the public schools there. He seems to have arrived here in about 1887. He spoke English well and served as a translator between Anglo employers and Chinese workers. He also worked as a ranch hand before he established his own vegetable farm in the Westminster area, selling his crop in Anaheim and Fullerton.

In 1896, he came to Santa Ana and opened a store on East Fourth Street where he sold Chinese and Japanese goods, including porcelain, silk and teas.

When the Spanish-American War began in 1898, Tow was vocal in his support of the American cause and tried to enlist in Company L, the local National Guard unit. The enlisting officers were inclined to dismiss him out of hand, but when they discovered he was a U.S. citizen and registered to vote, they took down his information. But to Tow's regret, Company L shipped out without him a few days later.

Undaunted, Tow volunteered for the United States Army and was sent to the Philippines in 1899. "The last thing he parted with before entering the services of the United States was his queue," the *Santa Ana Blade* reported. "He...is the first Chinaman to enlist in the service of the United States." Even before his enlistment, Tow received favorable notice in many of the local papers.

Tow remained in the Philippines after the war, married and had a family and became a successful Manila businessman. He died there sometime before 1940.

The most lurid incident in local Chinese history is the burning of Santa Ana's Chinatown in May 1906, after one of the residents, Wong Oe (sometimes identified as Wong Who Yee), was found to be suffering from leprosy. On the recommendation of the city board of health, the city council condemned the ramshackle wooden buildings and quarantined Wong Oe. The other six or eight remaining residents were allowed to remove their personal belongings (which were then fumigated) and horses, but all other livestock was ordered killed, and the vegetables stored there were destroyed.

On the night of May 25, 1906, a large crowd gathered as the local fire department set fire to the buildings, and in a matter of minutes, Santa Ana's Chinatown was no more.

Ching Wing, a Los Angeles merchant, came down as a representative of the Chinese consul in San Francisco. "The City Trustees have acted very fairly with the China boys," he told the *Santa Ana Blade*, "as they have provided tents for the sick man and the others and given them food, and have furthermore promised to recoup them for their loses by the burning of their homes. I was called here by a message that said there was likely to be serious trouble, but I found that there was no trouble at all."

Wong Oe died about ten days later. Some questioned whether he was actually suffering from leprosy. The Chinese Chamber of Commerce in Los Angeles arranged for Dr. Ralph Williams, a dermatologist, to examine the body. He said that the visible symptoms were inconclusive and suspected that it might be some other "loathsome disease," but later microscopic tests showed that it was indeed leprosy.

The displaced residents were soon moved to the Salvation Army hall on Sycamore Street. They initially threatened to sue the city over their loss of personal property (their homes and stores were all rented from an Anglo

Historian Merle Ramsey, who lived in Santa Ana at the time, claimed that this blurry image was a photo of the burning of Chinatown there in 1906. *Courtesy the First American Corporation.*

A postcard view of the Chungking Café on Center Street (now Lincoln Avenue) in downtown Anaheim, circa 1954. Owners Yet Lin (1903–1969) and his wife, Moey, are on the right. *Courtesy the Orange County Archives.*

property owner) but in the end accepted $100. The city also arranged for them to move to a piece of farmland southwest of town, along the Santa Ana River, where they could continue to grow vegetables for sale. Others chose to move away; storekeeper Yick Sing moved to Orange, where he was a prominent resident until his death in 1919. The last resident of the "China gardens" along the river moved out in 1923.

The smuggling operations that crossed Orange County formed the other Chinese controversy in the early 1900s. Laws against Chinese immigration were still tight, so men determined to enter the United States usually went to Baja California first and then were brought up by boat. The mouth of San Mateo Creek, at the southern tip of Orange County, was a popular landing spot around 1910. There, they were met by men who led them across the O'Neill Ranch beyond El Toro, where autos would pick them up and drive them to Los Angeles. Others came in to Santa Ana and took the Pacific Electric cars north.

Curiously, some of these men were brought here to be trained as soldiers and then were smuggled back into China to fight in the 1911 revolution that removed the dowager empress and made Dr. Sun Yat-Sen the first president of the new Chinese republic.

The last of Orange County's pioneer Chinese immigrants passed away in the mid-1930s, but there were a few other Chinese families who had moved here by then. Herbalist Harry Chan came to Santa Ana in about 1930 and operated a shop there for more than a quarter of a century. Kuey Quon opened his Jade Tree gift shop in Laguna Beach in 1937. Other Chinese residents had restaurants or worked as household servants.

The first prominent Chinese restaurant in Orange County was the Chungking Café on East Lincoln Avenue in downtown Anaheim. It opened in 1929 as Nicco Chop Suey and was run by a Japanese family named Fujii in the 1930s. With the relocation of the Japanese during World War II, the restaurant passed into Chinese hands. In about 1950, Yet C. Lin and his wife took over. Besides Chinese and American dishes, they also offered two banquet rooms, a gift shop and takeout service and managed a staff of forty.

The number of Chinese Americans here remained small until the 1970s. As late as 1960, there were still fewer than 500 Chinese residents in Orange County. The 1980 census found 14,500 people of Chinese origin here; by 2010, that number had grown to nearly 80,000. It would be interesting to know if any of them are descended from our early Chinese pioneers.

# RED CARS IN AN ORANGE COUNTY

It has become almost a legend—the Pacific Electric Railway, the Big Red Cars. At one time, the Pacific Electric boasted more than one thousand miles of track and 2,500 trains a day running from Redlands to Canoga Park and from Long Beach all the way up the slopes of Mount Lowe. It provided convenient, inexpensive and fairly comfortable service to hundreds of communities throughout Southern California. People commuted daily to work or school, took the cars into Los Angeles for big shopping trips or went down to the beach for summer vacations. Passengers from Balboa, Santa Ana or Yorba Linda could be in downtown Los Angeles in about an hour and a half.

For more than forty years, the Pacific Electric played an important role in the development of Orange County, and quite a few of our local communities owe their founding, growth or incorporation to the arrival of the "PE."

The Pacific Electric was a regional transportation system, designed to tie all of Southern California together with a single electric trolley car system. The company was organized in Los Angeles in 1901 by Henry E. Huntington, a nephew of pioneer railroad builder Collis P. Huntington. He and his partners began buying up existing trolley lines and street railroads and building their own tracks to connect them all together.

The Southern Pacific railroad saw the benefits of Huntington's growing trolley system, and by 1911, it had acquired control of the company. Now the PE cars were able to make use of the Southern Pacific's tracks as well, and SP freight was hauled along the PE lines.

# BEACH TOWNS

The Pacific Electric built three major branch lines into Orange County. The first was the Newport-Balboa "surf line," which followed the coast down from Long Beach. About the time construction began in 1903, the new town of Bay City was laid out. It was renamed Seal Beach in 1913 and incorporated two years later.

Except for the tracks of the Pacific Electric, Seal Beach was largely cut off from the rest of Orange County by Anaheim Bay. At times, some residents even toyed with the idea of annexing to Los Angeles County. In the summer, tourists poured into town on the PE. In the 1910s and '20s, the most popular destination was the Joy Zone at the foot of the pier. A number of the attractions came from the Panama-Pacific International Exhibition, held in San Francisco in 1915 to celebrate the opening of the Panama Canal. Visitors could ride the roller coaster, eat at the Jewel City Café and watch the dancing lights at the end of the pier at night.

In 1904, as passenger service began on the surf line, Sunset Beach was laid out below Anaheim Bay. It remained its own little beachfront community until 2011, when it was finally annexed to Huntington Beach.

Next on the line was Pacific City, laid out in 1901 by the West Coast Land & Water Company. Most of the tract was still unsold two years later when Huntington and his partners bought out the land and water company and renamed the town Huntington Beach. The first Pacific Electric cars arrived there in June 1904. Incorporated in 1909, the city remained primarily a vacation town until oil was discovered in 1920.

In August 1905, service began to Newport Beach. Two new tracts—East Newport and Balboa, with its distinctive pavilion—had already been laid out in anticipation of the PE's arrival, along with a number of new subdivisions. Once again, Huntington and his associates invested in local real estate, including buying the mudflats that would one day become Lido Isle.

Bay Island was the first of the local islands to be developed, beginning in 1903. It was the only natural island in the bay. The others were raised by dredging up sand from the bottom of the bay, starting with Balboa and Collins Islands in 1906. Ferry service to Balboa Island began in 1909 and continues to this day.

For decades, Newport boosters lobbied for government aid to dredge and improve the bay. There was some debate whether it would be developed as a commercial port or a pleasure harbor, but in the end, the yachting and

The Joy Zone at the foot of the Seal Beach pier, circa 1920, featured food, sideshow attractions, carnival games, a bowling alley, a dance hall and an impressive wooden roller coaster. All were gone by the mid-1930s. *Courtesy the Orange County Archives.*

The first Pacific Electric excursion car reached Huntington Beach in June 1904. The little open-air depot is on the right. *Courtesy the Center for Oral and Public History, Cal State Fullerton.*

sailboat crowd won out. More dredging and expanded jetties were finally completed in 1936.

While Newport Beach had its wharf, fishing fleet and canneries, Balboa was always a tourist destination, with a tiny downtown running from its pleasure pier to the Pavilion, where music and dancing filled the summer nights. During the Prohibition era, Balboa enjoyed a reputation as a "wide open" town where liquor and gambling were easy to find.

The Pacific Electric hoped to bridge the mouth of Newport Harbor and continue on down the coast. George Hart laid out the town of Corona

del Mar along the proposed right-of-way in 1904, but the tracks never got beyond Balboa, which they reached on July 4, 1906.

That same year, the city of Newport Beach incorporated. The community claimed seven hundred residents but could only muster fifty-six voters when the incorporation election was held on August 21, 1906. It took in East Newport, Balboa, and what would become Lido Isle. Corona del Mar did not become a part of the city until 1923, in part so it could connect to the city water system.

# ON TO SANTA ANA

The next Pacific Electric branch into Orange County was the Santa Ana line, which was completed in November 1905. It left the L.A.–Long Beach line at Watts and entered Orange County near Crescent and Moody, angling southeast. Much of the right-of-way is still intact. It crossed Beach Boulevard just north of Katella and Garden Grove Boulevard just west of Euclid, reaching Fourth Street in Santa Ana just east of Fairview.

Once again, new towns sprang up along the tracks. Cypress and Benedict (later renamed Stanton) were both laid out in 1905. Garden Grove also got a boost when the Big Red Cars came to town, and several new subdivisions were laid out on the west side of Santa Ana along the tracks.

Cypress had another interesting connection to the Pacific Electric. It was founded by S.O. "Sam" Walker, a big local landowner and a major political powerbroker at the time. In fact, he was the Southern Pacific's main man in Orange County in the days when the railroad wielded enormous power in the state. The tiny townsite was located at the northwest corner of Walker Street (named for its founder) and Lincoln Avenue.

Even with a connection to the Pacific Electric, the new town of Benedict remained largely rural. So, when the City of Anaheim was looking for a site for a new sewage treatment plant in 1911, it looked to the farmlands southwest of town. The city quietly obtained an option on the J.M. Gilbert Ranch, near Cerritos and Magnolia. When the word leaked out, the local ranchers were not pleased. They didn't want a "sewer farm" in their backyard.

One of the big landowners in the area was Orange County developer Phil Stanton. Stanton was a prominent California politician at the time, having just finished a term as speaker of the California Assembly, and recently lost the Republican nomination for governor to Hiram Johnson. He believed that no city had the right to impose something like a sewer farm on an area that didn't want it, so he joined the local ranchers in their struggle.

Stanton met with the Anaheim city officials and even offered part of his own ranch, west of town on Brookhurst, as a site for the treatment plant. He said that he could absorb the loss in property value it would bring, unlike the small ranchers around Benedict. But the city was adamant—it wanted the Gilbert Ranch.

So, Stanton suggested a new idea: if the ranchers would incorporate as a city, they could block Anaheim's sewer farm plans. When the petition drive began, the ranchers decided to name their new city after their benefactor. The incorporation election was held May 23, 1911, and drew about a 90

*Left*: A souvenir ribbon from "El Dia de los Carros," marking the official arrival of the Pacific Electric in Santa Ana on November 22, 1905. The Parade of Products through downtown continued as an annual event for several more years. *Author's collection*.

*Below*: The Pacific Electric tracks slice through downtown Garden Grove, circa 1910. Notice the electric poles all along the line. The two-story Garden Grove Hotel near the center of the photo stood at the corner of Euclid Avenue and Garden Grove Boulevard from the 1880s until the 1920s. *Courtesy the Orange County Archives*.

percent turnout. The measure carried, seventy-six to sixty-five. At about ten square miles, Stanton was suddenly the largest city (in area) in all of Orange County despite having a population of only about 750.

One of the first acts of the new city council was to ban sewer farms in the city limits. But the City of Anaheim would not be deterred. As opposition grew, Mr. Gilbert tried to back out of the option, but the city forced him to complete the sale. It then turned to the courts, seeking to have the incorporation election overturned, but it was no use. Eventually, the city gave up. And so did Stanton. In 1921, with the threat safely past, the City of Stanton voted to disincorporate. It would be thirty-five years before the city incorporated again.

Stanton's story is not unique. In 1921, residents of the Orangethorpe area, between Anaheim and Fullerton, learned that the City of Fullerton was eying their area for a sewer farm. Following Stanton's lead, they voted to incorporate as the city of Orangethorpe. Two years later, after plans were dropped, the city disincorporated. But unlike Stanton, Orangethorpe never revived.

# TO THE NORTH

To the north, the La Habra–Yorba Linda branch entered the county from Whittier, running between La Habra Boulevard and Lambert. It jogged south at Harbor and again beyond State College. The Imperial Highway now follows that last leg of the line southeast into Yorba Linda.

Like the coast line, the northern line was built in stages, reaching La Habra in 1908, Brea in 1910 and Yorba Linda—laid out in anticipation of the line—in 1911. Plans called to eventually continue out the Santa Ana Canyon and connect with the PE's inland line to Riverside, but the extension was never built.

La Habra and Yorba Linda were primarily agricultural communities in the early days, but Brea was an oil town. Wildcatters had been putting down wells in the Puente Hills/Brea Canyon area since the 1860s, and a few were pumping by the 1880s, but the first important strike in the area was at Olinda, in Carbon Canyon, in 1897. A little town soon grew up there, with a school, stores and churches.

Down in the valley, W.J. Hole—the founder of La Habra—convinced Henry Huntington and others to back a new townsite (no doubt in

The Pacific Electric depot in La Habra, circa 1915, with the passenger area on the left and the freight house and loading platform on the right. *Courtesy the Orange County Archives.*

anticipation that the PE would arrive someday). In 1903, the town of Randolph was laid out, named for Epes Randolph, the general manager of the Pacific Electric. A school district was formed, but the town never took off, and the tract map wasn't even filed with the county until 1908. By then, Epes Randolph had left the company, and in January 1911, a new map was filed changing the name to Brea.

## OTHER LINES

The Pacific Electric built three shorter lines in Orange County as well. One of its first purchases back in 1901 was the old Santa Ana & Orange Motor line—although the old steam-powered cars were not replaced by electric trolleys until 1914, when the tracks were moved from South Glassell Street in downtown Orange to Lemon Street. The PE tracks were also extended up into the city's packing house district, for freight shipments.

In 1909, the Pacific Electric built a small connector line between Santa Ana and Huntington Beach. It was primarily a freight line, but it did provide

The Pacific Electric bridge over Harbor Boulevard was a local landmark from 1917 until it was demolished in 1964. The other side of the bridge read, "Welcome to Fullerton." It is shown here in 1937 during a railfan excursion along the PE. *Courtesy the Fullerton Public Library.*

A double PE passenger car bound for Los Angeles rolls down West Fourth Street in Santa Ana in the early 1920s. *Courtesy the First American Corporation.*

some passenger service to the little towns of Greenville and Talbert (now Fountain Valley) until 1922.

The PE's last major project in Orange County was a small line from La Habra down across the Bastanchury Ranch to Fullerton, which opened in 1917. It had hoped to push south to Anaheim, but World War I intervened, and Anaheim remained the only large community in Orange County without a PE connection.

The Pacific Electric hit its peak in the mid-1920s and then began a long decline. Despite persistent rumors, the PE was not secretly bought out by "the automobile interests"; it simply ceased to be a moneymaking operation. Its demise was long, slow and perhaps inevitable. Good roads and cheap automobiles reduced both passenger and freight traffic. The depression of the 1930s also cut into its profits, and the PE started to abandon its less profitable lines. Passenger service to Orange ended in 1930 and was replaced by buses from the PE's own Motor Transit bus company. The La Habra–Yorba Linda line, along with the Fullerton cutoff, shut down passenger service in 1938.

Then came World War II, gas and tire rationing, as well as Southern Californians taking jobs at distant war work plants and military bases. Ridership increased, but the PE was unable to expand or replace its aging trolley cars.

After the war, the shutdowns continued. The Newport-Balboa and Santa Ana lines both closed within days of each other in 1950, ending all passenger service in Orange County. The last line to close was the first to have opened—the Los Angeles–Long Beach line, in 1961. The old right-of-way was reborn in 1990 as the Blue Line, the first of Southern California's modern light rail lines, proving that history does sometimes repeat itself.

# KING CITRUS AND QUEEN VALENCIA

Once upon a time in Orange County, money grew on trees. Seventy-five years ago, much of central Orange County was one vast orchard, dotted with little towns. Citrus trees cascaded in green and gold out of the foothills and along the rich coastal plain in neat, orderly rows, divided by windbreaks of eucalyptus trees. The citrus industry fueled the local economy for decades, creating an easterner's image of paradise: a sunny, fertile land where health and wealth grew on trees.

It was the Spanish missionaries who brought the first oranges to California in the 1790s. The first local plantings seem to have been made by the Yorba family around their adobes at Olive and in the Santa Ana Canyon, perhaps as early as the 1850s. By 1870, seedling trees joined the vineyards at Anaheim, and the first large orchard was set out near Orange in 1873.

Grapes and grain were still the big crops here in the 1870s. While the soil and climate allowed citrus to thrive, irrigation water was limited and there was no good way to ship the fruit to distant markets. But in the 1880s, a blight devastated the local vineyards, and railroad competition drove down freight rates, prompting more and more ranchers to turn to citrus. By 1889, there were more than 400,000 citrus trees growing in Orange County.

Mediterranean Sweets, St. Michaels and Malta Bloods were popular varieties in the early days, but each had their drawbacks. "The Malta Blood did not have much appeal because the meat had blotches of red that looked like blood stains," longtime Placentia grower George Key wrote. "The St. Michaels were small with a lot of seeds."

Ross and Duffill's Dos Pinos Grove ranch—shown here in about 1900—included their own private packing house. The ranch was located on Valencia Drive, between Acacia Avenue and State College Boulevard, which was considered part of Placentia at the time but is now in the city of Fullerton. This photo was later used on one of their citrus labels. *Courtesy the First American Corporation.*

The seedless, winter-ripening Washington navel was introduced in Riverside in 1873. The spring-ripening Valencia was first imported to Southern California in 1876 by A.B. Chapman (one of the founders of Orange) to his San Gabriel Valley ranch, and the Southern California Semi-Tropical Fruit Company planted the first local grove in 1880 on what is now the Cal State Fullerton campus. Fullerton's first mayor, Charles C. Chapman (the namesake of Chapman University), helped to establish a market for Valencias in the 1890s by insisting on shipping only the highest-quality fruit to the East.

Washington navels proved to do better inland and were only a small percentage of the plantings here. By 1915, there were already nearly 20,000 acres of Valencias in Orange County, and only 940 acres of navels. Other ranchers grew lemons (mostly Eurekas), and a few planted grapefruit, limes and tangerines. Valencias begin ripening in April, and with care, they can be picked as late as October or even November. By that time, the navel harvest has begun, providing almost a year-round supply of fresh fruit.

Citrus officials gather in 1934 to honor pioneer Valencia grower Richard Gilman as the Native Daughters of the Golden West dedicate a monument in honor of the first commercial Valencia grove here, which he planted in 1880. The concrete pillar is gone, but the plaque can still be found on the campus of Cal State Fullerton. The men are toasting Gilman (second from the left) with—what else?—orange juice. *Courtesy the Old Orange County Courthouse Museum.*

Unlike some other parts of the Citrus Belt, most of the citrus ranches in central and northern Orange County were small, ten- to twenty-acre family operations. This created a very middle-class society, with modest homes scattered throughout the groves.

The groves meant work for more than just the growers. There were fumigators, pickers, teamsters, packers, cement irrigation pipe manufacturers, tractor dealers and sundry other tradesmen living off the wealth of the groves. For example, the *Orange City Directory* for 1919 shows perhaps one-third of the local workforce employed in some aspect of the citrus industry.

By 1925, there were more than 44,000 acres of citrus in Orange County. By 1936, when Orange County supplied one-sixth of the nation's Valencia crop, there were 66,000 acres. The peak year was 1948, with 77,082 acres planted to citrus here—nearly 6 million trees.

# INSECT PESTS AND COMMISSION AGENTS

Citrus farming is not without its problems, though. The trees are delicate (some early growers describe young groves as being "kept like a garden") and easily damaged by frost and a variety of insect pests. Red, black, white and even purple "scale"—a microscopic parasite—were the biggest problem in the early days. They were attacked by fumigation and the use of ladybugs, which feed on the scale.

But fumigation had its own problems. The cyanide gas used was so harsh that the leaves would burn in the sun, so heavy tents had to be hoisted over the trees before the poisonous gas was released. Another group of local growers tried to patent the idea of simply doing their fumigation at night. Eventually, spraying replaced fumigation altogether. Other diseases were avoided by grafting. Sweet oranges were grafted onto "sour" rootstock, which was less susceptible to disease. But this would later lead to other problems.

As for frost, the early growers would simply set fires around the groves on cold nights. Later, oil-fueled "smudge pots" were used. In some citrus towns, the fire bell would ring as freezing weather approached. Later, radio stations carried frost warnings. In either case, it meant a long, cold, sooty night for local growers. The most famous freeze was in 1913, when temperatures fell to a reported eighteen degrees in some areas. Another bad year was 1937. Air quality complaints finally forced the elimination of smudging in the 1950s. Instead, large fans were installed to keep air circulating, so the cold could not settle in on the groves.

Citrus growing was also a patient man's game. The seedlings were normally started in seedbeds and then transplanted to the groves when about one year old, with plenty of space left around them for future growth. Then it could be five or six years until the trees started producing a crop—and several years more before they would turn a profit.

In the meantime, ranchers would grow other crops between the rows of young trees (tomatoes were especially popular), work for other ranchers or hold down full-time jobs while waiting for their grove to come into bearing. But once it did, a healthy tree might produce eight hundred pounds of fruit or more each year for forty or fifty years. This was a long-term investment that forced the growers to stick with it through good years and bad.

Another major problem in the nineteenth century was selling the crop. Early growers had only two options—pick, pack, ship and market their own fruit (packing on their ranch or in small, private packing houses) or sell their

The Orange County Department of Agriculture hosted an orchard heater demonstration in 1950, showing off various designs. By then, smudge pots were falling out of favor and would eventually be replaced by wind machines here. *Courtesy the Old Orange County Courthouse Museum.*

crop while still on the trees to commission agents from the big wholesale produce distributors.

The problem was that the wholesalers got to determine how much fruit was saleable, and growers had to rely on their figures for how much fruit was spoiled in shipping and what prices it earned in the East. "And it got to be—if you want it politely—so many robbers," one early grower recalled.

In self-defense, some of the growers in Southern California banded together to pack and sell their own fruit. The Orange Growers Protective Union, founded in 1885, was the first attempt to combat the commission agents. They contracted with their own wholesaler and sent two agents east to keep an eye on things (Dr. O.P. Chubb of Orange was one of them). Naturally the commission agents weren't pleased, and the Union faded away after a few years.

It was not until 1893 that a successful citrus grower's organization came along: the Southern California Fruit Exchange.

# Into the Packing House

The Southern California Fruit Exchange was built on a cooperative basis. Local growers would come together to form a packing house association to pick and pack their fruit. Several local packing houses would then form a district fruit exchange to coordinate sales and shipping. The growers would elect a board of directors to hire a manager and run the packing house. The packing house boards would then select a director for the local fruit exchange. And the fruit exchange boards each had a representative on the board of the Southern California Fruit Exchange.

The Southern California Fruit Exchange coordinated efforts among its members, purchased orchard and packing house supplies in bulk and handled the marketing that transformed oranges from a specialty crop into an everyday commodity. "Oranges for Health—California for Wealth," it proclaimed in advertisements across the nation. In 1907, it also coined a new trademark: Sunkist. Over the years, it became so closely associated with the organization that in 1952, it changed its name to Sunkist Growers Inc.

"Just like any other business," recalled Harold Brewer, the second president of the Villa Park Orchards Association, "a group can do business cheaper than a single individual. The picking was co-operatively done. The hauling was done by the packing houses—they were still hauling with teams of horses when I came over here. All of these—and the packing—were much cheaper than having somebody in the business to make a profit to do it. That profit was divided back to the growers."

The Fruit Growers Supply Company (a wholly owned subsidiary of Sunkist) was established in 1907 to keep prices down through bulk buying. It eventually owned not only its own lumber mill but also its own forest tracts in Northern California, just to supply wood for orange crates.

The cooperative model was soon adopted for other grower needs. Local water companies such as the Santa Ana Valley Irrigation Company (SAVI) and the Anaheim Union Water Company had long been run on a nonprofit, stockholder basis. They were later joined by dozens of other water companies, big and small. Some of the little mutual water companies had only a single well, shared by several growers. Cooperative fumigation and pest control companies were also established by local growers.

By the 1920s, Sunkist was handling 75 percent of California's citrus crop. But it was not the only grower's association. The Mutual Orange Distributors association (MOD) was organized in Redlands in 1906 and shipped its best fruit under the Pure Gold label. American Fruit Growers ran a poor third with its Blue Goose label. It had only three packing houses in Orange County—in Fullerton, Orange and San Juan Capistrano.

The first commercial packing house in what is now Orange County opened in Orange in 1883. It was a private company that handled all sorts of fruit year round. The first cooperative packing house in Orange County was also in Orange—the Santiago Orange Growers Association, formed in 1893. It was quickly followed by associations in Placentia, Tustin, Fullerton and Anaheim.

By 1905, there were eighteen packing houses in Orange County—six in Fullerton, five in Santa Ana, four in Orange, two in Anaheim and one at McPherson—although only a few of them were devoted entirely to citrus. Most of them handled both oranges and lemons, but as the years went on, they began to specialize, and several lemon packing houses were established here.

At the peak, in the early 1940s, forty-five packing houses were operating in Orange County. There was the Anaheim Orange and Lemon Association, the Garden Grove Citrus Association, the Bradford Brothers in Placentia, Goldenwest Citrus in Tustin, the Olive Hillside Growers, McPherson Heights and dozens of other plants. These packing houses handled millions of pounds of fruit. In 1929, for example, Santiago Orange Growers in Orange handled some 60 million pounds of fruit—two thousand railroad cars full—making it the biggest Valencia house in the country.

Although the equipment changed over the years, the basic packing house process has never varied. Picking crews were sent out by the packing houses on a schedule coordinated with the local member-growers. After about 1910, the crews were largely made up of Mexican American workers (many of them recent immigrants). Some packing houses had their own worker camps to house seasonal employees.

Picking was precise work. The fruit had to be clipped off the branches with just enough stem left (too much and it would damage other fruit, but if it was removed entirely, it left the orange liable to spoil). The pickers climbed tall ladders with canvas bags over their shoulders. The bags were emptied into wooden field boxes that held sixty to seventy pounds of fruit. Sal Martinez, who came to Orange in 1919, recalled the strict rules for pickers:

> *They used to deduct you for long stems, short stems, slant stems, a clipper cut, pulling, slack boxes, they'd deduct you a quarter of a cent. They used to pay you every two weeks, so they'd deduct you for all the boxes you had picked during those two weeks…There used to be an inspector, he'd come and inspect you…and they had a state inspector, he'd come about once a*

Inside the Santiago Orange Growers Association packing house in Orange, 1932, showing the rows of packing tables in the foreground and the graders working overhead in the background. *Author's collection*.

The Foothill Groves packing house in Yorba Linda, circa 1924, was a member of the Mutual Orange Distributors association. It was located along the Pacific Electric tracks on what would become the Imperial Highway. Notice the many skylights angling across the roof. *Courtesy the Orange County Archives*.

A Mexican American picking crew pauses for a portrait on the Hewes Ranch, along the base of the foothills between Orange and Tustin, circa 1925. The picking bags on their shoulders could be opened at the bottom to empty the fruit into wooden field boxes. *Courtesy the First American Corporation.*

*month. But the regular house inspector, he'd inspect you six or seven times in that two-week period. Oh, they were strict! If they inspected you once, and you had a bad orange, they counted it for two. See the state inspector would inspect all your box, but the house inspector he only inspected about half, so if he found one bad one it was counted for two.*

The field boxes would then be hauled to the packing house, where the fruit was scrubbed with soap and water and air-dried. In later years, a light coat of wax was then added. Greenish fruit that was otherwise ripe was "sweated" by exposing it to ethylene gas—this gave it the nice orange hue that shoppers expected.

Conveyor belts moved the fruit through the packing house. Women graders sorted the fruit by size, shape and color. Then it rolled down to the packers. The top grades were individually wrapped in tissue paper and packed into wooden crates. Wrapping the fruit was first introduced in Orange in about 1880 by pioneer citrus grower A.B. Clark. Printing directly on the fruit began in the 1920s, but printed wrappers continued to be used on the best grades until the 1940s. Lower grades were packed more simply or even sold in bulk to "product" companies such as TreeSweet (founded in Santa Ana in 1933) that turned them into juice, jam or animal food.

The sealed crates were then sent off to the pre-cooler to chill the fruit before it was loaded into railroad cars (all of the packing houses had their own railroad spurs). Ice was packed into the front of the cars in the early days, where air could blow across it to help keep the fruit cool on its long journey east. Later, refrigerated cars were used.

Until the introduction of cardboard orange crates in the mid-1950s, each crate had a distinctive lithographed label pasted on both ends. Most featured idyllic scenes of Southern California or lovely maidens holding up oranges or promoted their place of origin. There were brands like Rooster, Bird Rocks, Cleopatra, Atlas, Jim Dandy and any of a hundred others. Each was unique, all were eye-catching and some were genuinely beautiful.

*Opposite, top*: Orange packers hard at work in the Yorba Linda Citrus Association packing house, circa 1949. Conveyor belts brought the fruit to the women, who had to stay on their feet throughout their shift. *Courtesy the Orange County Archives.*

*Opposite, bottom*: SweeTreat brand, from Santiago Orange Growers in Orange (circa 1940), was a lower grade of oranges but still carried an attractive label. *Courtesy the Orange Public Library and History Center.*

Yet shoppers seldom saw these famous citrus labels. They were designed to help bidders at wholesale auction houses in New York, Chicago, St. Louis and other major cities. They knew which brands were the top grade from each packing house and which were field run. The colorful labels allowed the buyers to instantly spot the fruit they were looking for, even across a crowded room.

The district fruit exchanges coordinated shipping to prevent too much fruit being sent to one part of the country and not enough to another, ensuring every grower the best possible price. The Orange County Fruit Exchange (headquartered in Orange) operated from 1893 to 1995. The Northern Orange County Fruit Exchange in Anaheim served growers from 1917 to 1955. The Placentia Orange County Exchange operated from 1935 to 1978.

The packing house associations kept track of how much fruit came in from each member-grower, how it was graded and how much was sold. The returns were paid out every few weeks during the season in a series of "pools" divided among all the growers. Local merchants also waited for the pools to pay out, when many a grower would come in and settle up their accounts. Other growers took out crop loans with local banks, to be paid off at the end of every season.

## A Namesake Crop

The rise of citrus as Orange County's dominant crop began in the 1890s. While sugar beets, lima beans, walnuts and, later, avocados were an important part of the local economy, grapes, apricots, apples, celery and dozens of other crops faded. In 1930, citrus brought in more than $41 million in sales—80 percent of the county's agricultural income—while lima beans earned only $2.7 million, walnuts $1.7 million and sugar beets a mere $392,000.

Harold Brewer (1891–1990), a nephew of pioneer Valencia grower R.H. Gilman, came to Villa Park in 1923. "As far as the area was concerned," he recalled, "almost all of it was in citrus."

*You'd drive along the streets, and about all you'd see was a citrus grove and maybe a house on the corner or maybe long driveways leading back into a home. There were windbreaks to protect the orchards from the Santa*

Orange groves spread across the Irvine Ranch, circa 1956. A line of eucalyptus trees forms a windbreak across the center of the photo, with Old Saddleback visible in the distance. *Courtesy the Orange Public Library and History Center.*

> *Ana Winds—the "Devil Winds," they called them. You could drive to town and meet maybe one or two horse-and-buggies, or automobiles. Villa Park had no "town," except there was a little store at Villa Park Road and Wanda.*

When Brewer bought his grove in 1923, the trees were only a year old. For the next half-dozen years, he raised tomatoes and corn, often picking and selling them himself. He also did orchard work for other ranchers, while still tending his own young trees. When they finally came into full bearing, he began a pattern that continued for more than forty years:

> *The blooming was in the spring—April, May—and you did your irrigation and cultivation. Valencias were a crop that had ripe fruit and blossoms for the next year's crop at the same time, so that in this season you would have the picking of the crop that was formed the season before. Along in the fall, then, you would either fumigate or spray—fumigating for red scale and spiders, or spraying with oil sprays.*

*Then by the middle of fall your crop was all picked and you mostly irrigated, cultivated it up and sowed a cover crop, either clover or mustard or something to grow in the winter to make a mulch for the spring to work into the soil to help build it up.*

*Then during the winter, if you were in an area like I had in my lower acres here when it got cold, you had to watch the thermometer and maybe once in a while light up some smudge pots. In later years, the smudge pots went out and wind machines went in.*

*Then in the spring, you disked up* [the soil] *with a tractor and worked in this cover crop you'd grown through the winter.*

To celebrate the success of the local citrus industry, Anaheim hosted the California Valencia Orange Show from 1921 to 1931, with elaborate displays of citrus fruit, packing contests and all the trappings of a county fair. Over in Orange, the Queen Valencia Pageant was held from 1927 to 1930, with music and dance from the local high school students. The highlight of the evening was the crowning of Queen Valencia and her court, which included the Goddess of Spring and the Goddess of Southern California. Nearly ten thousand people attended the first year.

But the coming of the Depression marked the end of these celebrations. While the citrus market kept ahead of the economic decline for the first few years, by 1931 prices had fallen, sometimes leaving growers with trees full of fruit that wouldn't bring in enough to cover the costs of picking, packing and shipping. The Bastanchury Ranch between Fullerton and La Habra once boasted the largest citrus grove in the nation—some 2,500 acres, along with two private packing houses. But during the Depression, the family went bankrupt, and much of the land was sold to become Sunny Hills.

Labor unrest also grew in the 1930s. Attempts were made to unionize the Mexican American citrus workers, and there were several small strikes. Then, on June 11, 1936, nearly three thousand pickers throughout Orange County walked off the job in the largest strike in the history of the citrus industry. The men wanted their base pay raised from twenty-seven cents per hour to forty cents (plus their per-box rate), better treatment from the field foremen (who could pretty much hire, fire and withhold salaries at will) and union recognition.

The strike dragged on for eight weeks. Strikers attacked replacement workers brought in to harvest the crop. Strike meetings were broken up by vigilantes, and law enforcement officers made mass arrests. But in the end, the pickers received only a small increase in pay and some changes in

The elaborate entrance to the California Valencia Orange Show in Anaheim, built in 1925. The fairgrounds were located on what is now the site of La Palma Park. *Courtesy the Anaheim Public Library.*

Queen Valencia and her court reigned over a pageant in downtown Orange in May 1930 to mark the start of the harvest season. *Author's collection.*

Orange pickers, with their tall ladders, work in a grove in Fullerton, circa 1930. Pickers were paid both hourly and by the box. *Courtesy the Orange County Archives.*

working conditions but no union recognition, and the strike left lingering violence and ill will on all sides.

When World War II began, growers again found themselves desperate for workers as thousands of men and women enlisted in the military or found jobs in defense plants. High school students were enlisted as pickers during off hours, workers were brought in from Jamaica and even German prisoners of war were sent to pick fruit, with a POW camp set up in Garden Grove.

The war years also saw the birth of the Bracero program, which brought up workers from Mexico each season to work in the groves. Between 1943, when the first Braceros reached Orange County, and 1958, nearly seventy thousand Mexican nationals passed through half a dozen local camps. The program continued until 1964.

# FADING BLOSSOMS

By then, the citrus industry here was in decline. A year after local acreage peaked in 1948, nearly seven thousand acres of orange trees were torn out. The postwar migration to Southern California had begun in earnest, and each year, more and more trees fell as housing tracts began to blanket Orange County. The tracts raised the value of local land—increasing property taxes for growers—and domestic water demands also raised prices on irrigation water.

A new disease also swept through the local groves in the 1940s and '50s. Known as the "Quick Decline," it attacked trees grafted to sour rootstock, killing them dead almost overnight. By 1961, more than 300,000 trees here had been lost to the Quick Decline. There is still no known cure.

Orange County lost about one-third of its total agricultural acreage in the 1950s, and in 1962—for the first time since records were kept—Valencia oranges were no longer our top agricultural income producer, slipping behind the dairy industry. By 1967, citrus had dropped to a humiliating fifth place, behind nursery stock and cut flowers, strawberries, the dairy industry and chicken eggs. By 1990, there was barely four thousand acres of citrus left here—most of it Valencias on the Irvine Ranch. Twenty years later, less than seventy-five acres of oranges survived.

One by one, the packing houses merged or closed up. Central Lemon in Villa Park—once the largest lemon packing houses in the state—voted to dissolve in 1960. Santiago Orange Growers packed its last crop in 1965. Goldenwest Citrus in Tustin closed down in 1968. By the early 1980s, only four packing houses remained. By then, computers were used to help grade the fruit, and Sunkist was experimenting with automatic packing machines that could fill about 150 boxes per hour.

The Villa Park Orchards Association was the last to go. Founded by local growers in 1912, it moved its operation to the old Santiago Orange Growers packing house in Orange in 1978 and operated there until 2006, when it moved to Ventura County.

The key to Villa Park's survival has been expansion. As other packing associations closed, Villa Park Orchards signed up the remaining growers. As early as 1959, it absorbed the Escondido Co-Operative Citrus Association, bringing in important San Diego County acreage. In 1962, it added its first grapefruit and tangerine growers in the Coachella Valley, allowing the packing house to remain active between orange packing seasons. Villa Park Orchards also helped open important new markets around the Pacific Rim, and its fruit can be found in markets and street stalls in Malaysia, Australia, Hong Kong, Singapore, Japan and Korea.

Today, even in Orange County, oranges are mostly found in grocery stores. But the impact of the citrus industry still survives.

# THE GOOD ROADS MOVEMENT

In the first few years of the twentieth century, it was clear that the "horseless carriage" was no longer just a novelty or an expensive toy; the automobile was here to stay. But to really be effective, an automobile needs paved roads. And so began the Good Roads movement.

The movement actually began by looking backward. For a number of years, there had been a growing interest in recognizing the old El Camino Real, the Royal Road that ran from mission to mission in Spanish times. The California Federation of Women's Clubs took up the issue in 1902, calling for the preservation of the route by making it a state highway. In 1904, the Los Angeles Chamber of Commerce called a convention to promote a highway along El Camino Real from San Diego to Santa Barbara, which led to the creation of the El Camino Real Association. Local "sections" were established throughout Southern California, including a chapter in Santa Ana in June 1904. The association worked with local officials, historians and surveyors to select a route that mirrored the historic Camino Real but was also practical as a modern roadway.

In 1910, California voters approved $18 million in highway construction bonds. One year later, Orange County submitted its recommendation for a route for our leg of the first state highway. It was essentially the Camino Real route selected a few years before, zigzagging from town to town. It entered the county on Whittier Boulevard, turning south on Harbor through Fullerton down to Anaheim, where it jogged over to Anaheim Boulevard and continued southeast to meet what is now Manchester Boulevard. The highway turned

County supervisors and South County leaders gather for a publicity photo for the Ortega Highway, 1930. *Left to right*: Supervisor George Jeffrey, Ferris Kelly and Carl Hankey of the San Juan Capistrano Chamber of Commerce, Laguna Beach mayor Frank Champion, William Griswold of San Juan Capistrano and Supervisor Willard Smith. *Courtesy the Orange County Archives.*

east at Chapman Avenue and then south on Main Street to First Street in Santa Ana, which carried it east to El Camino Real in Tustin. The rest of the highway basically followed the route of today's I-5 freeway.

In some communities, the highway ran right through downtown. Others had to satisfy themselves with a near miss—notably Orange, but also La Habra and El Toro. Orange lost even more ground in 1930, when the City of Santa Ana built the Santa Ana Boulevard cutoff (the route of the I-5 today) between West Chapman and North Main.

After some delays in acquiring the right-of-way, construction on the new state highway through Orange County began in 1914. Our section of the fifteen- to eighteen-foot-wide cement highway was dedicated in November 1915, and by 1916, the road was open all the way to San Diego. The forty-five miles through Orange County cost a little more than $500,000. A

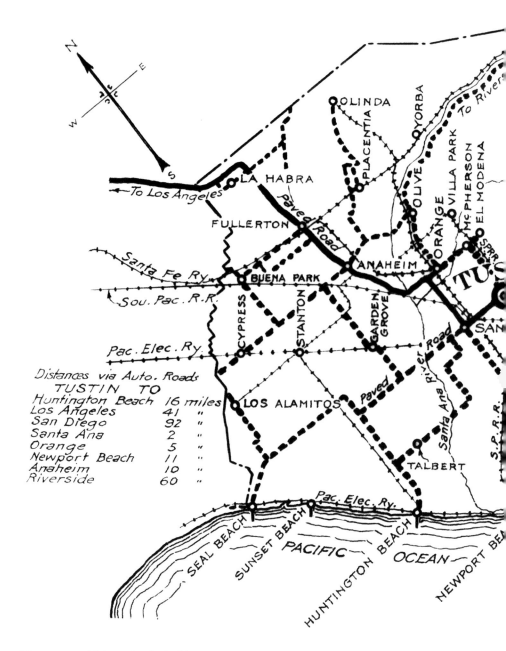

N
E
W
S

To Los Angeles

OLINDA
YORBA
To River
PLACENTIA
OLIVE
VILLA PARK
Mc PHERSON
EL MODENA
ORANGE

LA HABRA

FULLERTON

Paved Road

ANAHEIM

TU

Santa Fe Ry.

BUENA PARK

Sou. Pac. R.R.

SPRR

CYPRESS

STANTON

GARDEN GROVE

SAN

Pac. Elec. Ry.

Santa Ana River Road

S.P.R.R.

Distances via Auto. Roads
TUSTIN    TO
Huntington Beach   16 miles
Los Angeles        41   "
San Diego          92   "
Santa Ana           2   "
Orange              5   "
Newport Beach      11   "
Anaheim            10   "
Riverside          60   "

LOS ALAMITOS

Paved

TALBERT

Pac. Elec. Ry.

SEAL BEACH

SUNSET BEACH

PACIFIC

HUNTINGTON BEACH

OCEAN

NEWPORT BEA

The new state highway (marked with a solid line) gave Tustin a chance to portray itself as the center of Orange County. *Courtesy the Orange County Archives.*

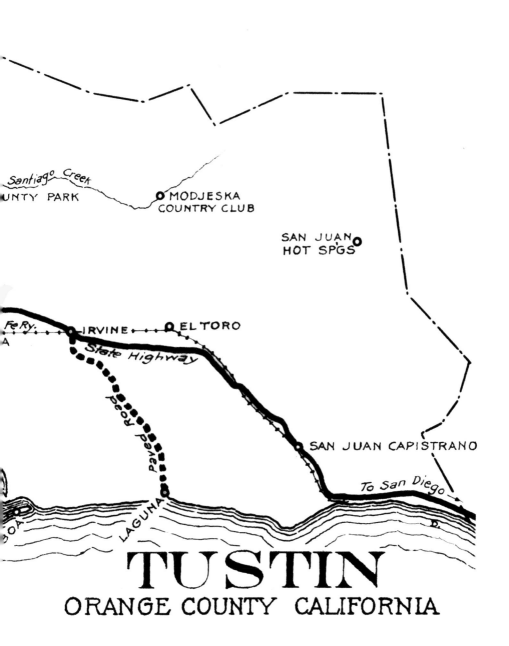

# TUSTIN
## ORANGE COUNTY CALIFORNIA

Looking north along State Highway 101 from Chapman Avenue, in West Orange, in 1938. This stretch was later replaced by the Santa Ana (I-5) Freeway. *Courtesy the Orange County Archives.*

number of the distinctive El Camino Real bells were placed along the route; a few of them still survive.

At the same time the state was gearing up its highway program, Orange County launched its own Good Roads project. In 1910, the board of supervisors appointed our first Highway Commission: W.H. Burnham of Orange, M.M. Crookshank of Santa Ana and C.C. Chapman of Fullerton, who soon resigned and was replaced by Judge Richard Egan of San Juan Capistrano. They proposed more than sixty miles of paving along what are still some of the county's major arterial routes, and in November 1912, county voters approved $1.27 million in highway bonds by a vote of 5,290 to 2,236. "The opposition was to bonding and not to the improvement of roads," former supervisor Sam Armor explained.

The first round of concrete paving, sixteen to twenty-two feet wide, was completed in March 1915 with money to spare, so more roads were added to the program. One of the most challenging projects was an auto road up the Santa Ana Canyon to Corona. By 1919, the county had completed 125 miles of paving, and local cities had added another 87 miles of cement.

## ALONG THE COAST

That same year, California voters approved a new $40 million highway bond, which included funds for a coast highway from Oxnard to San Juan Capistrano, where it would meet the existing state highway to San Diego.

The Coast Highway had long been a dream of beachfront residents and promoters. The county had already built a few stretches—notably from Seal Beach to Huntington Beach in 1916. Now with state money behind it, work continued in stages down the coast. With the opening of a long bridge across the mouth of the Santa Ana River in 1925, the two-lane concrete highway was open to traffic from Seal Beach to Newport Beach. A year later, Laguna Beach celebrated the arrival of the highway with a parade down the coast, beauty queens and an allegorical pageant, "The Linking of the Beaches," featuring two of Hollywood's biggest stars— Mary Pickford and Douglas Fairbanks.

The *South Coast News* later recalled that

> *Mary Pickford played the role of "The Spirit of Progress," and Douglas Fairbanks was "Vulcan the Blacksmith." Miss Marjorie Gowan, chosen as "Miss Laguna Beach," by a committee of artists, traveled to Long Beach where she presented to Miss Long Beach a petition, asking that she intercede with the mayor and ask him to join the other towns in presenting a petition to The Spirit of Progress, which requested that the Laguna Beach link be joined to the chain of beaches. The ceremony was repeated at each community. Arriving at Laguna Beach, at a place in Boat Canyon, the party found the Laguna Beach school children, in costume, forming five closed and one open link. The mayors and the misses from each town were escorted to a raised dais, where The Spirit of Progress was holding court, by a herald of two flower girls. The petition was presented and The Spirit of Progress consulted with her "advisors,"* [State Highway] *Commissioner* [Nelson] *Edwards and Thomas B. Talbert, then president of the Board of Supervisors, who gave their consent. She then called upon Vulcan the Blacksmith to weld the Laguna Beach link to the Chain of Beaches. Following that act, The Spirit of Progress then declared the highway officially open.*

The coastal hills south of Laguna proved slow going, and it was not until 1929 that paving was completed all the way down the coast.

City, state and county officials gather to mark the opening of the Coast Highway from Long Beach to Laguna Beach in 1925. Joining them in the ribbon cutting for the new bridge across the Santa Ana River is Hollywood starlet Belle Bennett. *Courtesy the Old Orange County Courthouse Museum.*

The Coast Highway under construction south of Laguna Beach, circa 1926. The billboard on the right advertises Coast Royal, one of several tracts laid out around the time the highway went through. *Courtesy the First American Corporation.*

Promoter Sidney Woodruff (left) welcomes an enthusiastic crowd on January 15, 1927, opening day of sales for the new community of Dana Point. *Courtesy the Orange County Archives.*

The narrow strip of the original Coast Highway cuts through downtown Capistrano Beach in 1930. *Courtesy the Orange County Archives.*

The construction of the Coast Highway prompted the founding of several new communities along the way and gave a boost to the existing communities—notably Corona del Mar and San Clemente.

Dana Point was founded by a group of investors, with developer Sidney Woodruff as its frontman. Sales began in January 1927, and there were big plans for recreational facilities and other amenities. But few houses were built before the stock market crashed in 1929, and by 1939, the whole plan had fallen apart. The town was still only sparsely settled when the county began harbor construction there in the 1960s.

Capistrano Beach also got off to a slow start. It was founded in 1928 by Edward L. Doheny Jr., son of a pioneer Southern California oilman. "Ned" Doheny dreamed of an upscale resort community, with mansions built in lavish Spanish style, but in February 1929, he was found dead in his Los Angeles mansion, and only twenty-eight homes had been built by the time Depression hit.

Up the coast, Surfside Colony (as it was originally known) went on the market in 1929, and about 150 homes had been built there by 1932. Four years later, promoters were offering "private beach homes" for as little as $195 down.

## Over the Mountain

Another road that opened up new areas was the Ortega Highway, but it was a long time in coming.

The idea of a road over the Santa Ana Mountains from San Juan Capistrano to Lake Elsinore had been floated as early as 1903. An old stage road already connected Capistrano with San Juan Hot Springs, some fourteen miles up San Juan Creek. A rough wagon road also climbed up into the mountains from the Elsinore side.

Orange County improved the road to the hot springs in 1913, but work stopped when it reached the county line. From there, a "tortuous and dangerous road" (little more than a trail, really) continued over the mountain.

The project then stalled for almost a decade until about 1924, when boosters on both sides of the mountain began a new push. The San Juan Capistrano Chamber of Commerce led the charge on this side,

The Ortega Highway enters the Cleveland National Forest in San Juan Canyon, 1939.
*Courtesy the Cleveland National Forest.*

and the county again got behind the idea. But the Elsinore Chamber of Commerce had a tougher time winning the support of Riverside County officials, who argued that they would simply be building a road *out* of Riverside County.

Roads run both ways, the inland boosters reminded them, and they would bring people and prosperity inland as well. Still, it took another five years to secure all the necessary approvals from both counties, the state and the federal government (since the road passes through the Cleveland National Forest).

Orange County took the lead in 1929, authorizing $70,000 to start improving the road on this side of the mountain. In May, San Juan Capistrano hosted a big barbecue to mark the start of construction. During the ceremonies, Father St. John O'Sullivan of Mission San Juan Capistrano proposed that the new road be named the Ortega Highway in honor of José Francisco Ortega, who had served as the lead scout for the Portolá Expedition 160 years before. It probably didn't hurt that the wife of Orange County supervisor George Jeffrey—a major proponent of the project—was a descendant of Sergeant Ortega.

Groundbreaking for the Ortega Highway in May 1929 drew a host of community leaders and county officials to San Juan Hot Springs. *Foreground, left to right:* County Supervisors George Jeffrey, John Mitchell and Willard Smith; Father St. John O'Sullivan, pastor of Mission San Juan Capistrano; J.S. Malcolm, who was in charge of the event; Fred Stoffel, chairman of the San Juan Capistrano Chamber of Commerce's Road Committee; Supervisors William Schumacher and C.H. Chapman; J. Frank Burke, the editor of the *Santa Ana Register*; and Tom Talbert, president of the Orange County Coast Association. *Courtesy the Orange County Archives.*

Later that year, the two counties agreed to form a joint highway improvement district. Funding would come from both counties, taxes on the properties along the route and $225,000 from the state. It was not until Orange County offered to hand over any state funding it received to Riverside County that its board of supervisors finally agreed to the project.

Seventeen miles of new road were needed (six in Orange County and eleven in Riverside). There would be some sharp turns and steep grades in places, but the road would save a good sixty-five miles between Elsinore and the Capistrano. A key link was the new high-arched bridge at the narrows in San Juan Canyon, just above San Juan Hot Springs.

By mid-1932, the road was open to limited traffic. "To drive over the scenic highway at that time was quite an adventure," Elsinore newspaper editor Tom Hudson later recalled, "with many short detours where graders

The San Juan Creek bridge above San Juan Hot Springs was a key link in the new
Ortega Highway. Shown here in about 1930, it still carries traffic today. *Courtesy the
Orange County Archives.*

were still at work, and with an abundance of dust, as no provision had been made for paving the road." The official dedication ceremonies were held in August 1933 overlooking Lake Elsinore, but it was not until February 1934 that the road was oiled the entire way across the mountain. Soon after, the joint district was dissolved, and the road became a state highway.

# FROM THE DESERT TO THE SEA

In the northern part of the county, another group of boosters was pushing its own highway project. Trucks were replacing railroads as an important means of shipping produce and freight. Hoping to lure traffic from the rich farmlands of the Imperial Valley on its way to Los Angeles, in 1929, a group of civic boosters from Los Angeles, Orange and Riverside Counties formed the Imperial Highway Association. At the time, some two hundred miles of rock and hill, desert and valley and trail and rut lay between the desert and sea, with less than half of it paved.

The official route of the Imperial Highway was adopted in January 1931. At the suggestion of Bob Hayes, manger of the El Centro Chamber of Commerce, it followed the old Butterfield stage route across the desert and along today's Highway 79 from Warner Hot Springs to Temecula, where it headed on to Corona via Lake Elsinore and Temescal Canyon. There the road turned west down the Santa Ana Canyon on its way to Yorba Linda and La Habra and then across Los Angeles County to meet the sea at El Segundo. It was billed as the "cannon ball route"—a straight shot from the desert to the sea—but it still managed to wind its way through the cities where support for the plan was strongest.

For the next thirty years, the Imperial Highway Association lobbied the cities and counties along the route to build a continuous road, with uniform construction standards—one hundred feet wide, with gentle curves to allow for truck traffic. The association's slogan was "wide for safety, straight for speed."

The stretch from Yorba Linda to Brea (following the tracks of the Pacific Electric) opened in July 1937. Governor Frank Merriam cut the ribbon, and the Goodyear blimp dropped orange juice on the new roadway to christen it.

When construction on Prado Dam forced the relocation of the road from Corona into the Santa Ana Canyon, the association lobbied hard for

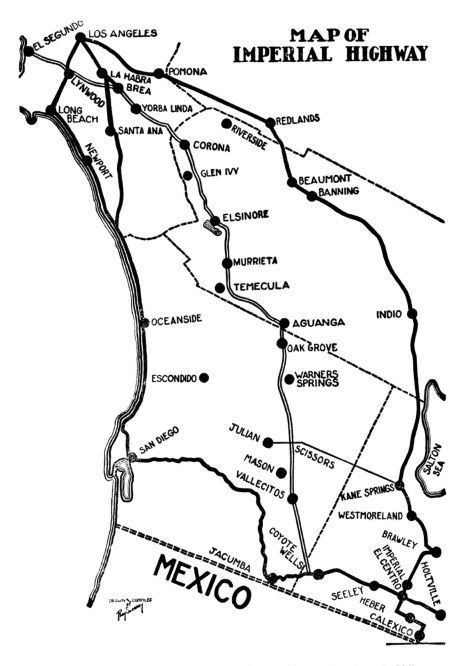

A 1936 map of the proposed Imperial Highway. It wound its way from Imperial Valley to the coast by way of Temecula, Corona, Yorba Linda and Brea. *Author's collection.*

improvements. The new road—completed in 1939—cut a mile off the drive from Corona to the top of the canyon and eliminated several sharp turns.

The stretch out of the canyon and into Yorba Linda was approved in 1952, but it was not until 1962 that the Yorba Linda Freeway (today's Richard Nixon Freeway) opened from Orangethorpe Avenue to Yorba Linda Boulevard. Originally built as an expressway, portions of it have since been upgraded to freeway status.

Orange County supplied its share of leadership to the Imperial Highway Association over the years. Brea trucking company owner Ed Peterkin was the first president. County supervisors Willard Smith, Leroy Lyon and Ralph McFadden also served as president, along with three Yorba Linda civic leaders—Phil Ton, Hurless Barton and Hoyt Corbit. Most prominent, though, was Yorba Linda rancher George Kellogg, who served as secretary from 1929 to 1975. He was a major voice for the association in the public press, and Kellogg Drive—which crosses the Imperial Highway—is named for him.

At its peak in the 1930s, the Imperial Highway Association could also boast its own monthly magazine, *The Butterfield Chronicle*, published from 1934 to 1939. One-time Anaheim printer and author Leonard Schwacofer served as editor and publisher.

Bit by bit, the route of the Imperial Highway was slowly transformed into a modern road. The last stretch was finally paved in 1961 near the San Diego/Imperial county line. With its original goal met, the Imperial Highway Association turned its attention to other highway improvements and even freeway projects. It survived on into the 1980s before finally disbanding.

Today, a few stretches of the old route in Los Angeles and Orange Counties still carry the Imperial Highway name, but its promoters are all but forgotten.

# THE GREAT DEPRESSION IN ORANGE COUNTY

You all know the story. In 1929, the stock market crashed, and within days, apple sellers were jostling for space on the sidewalks with folks in line for soup kitchens. Then Franklin Roosevelt came along, introduced a flurry of new federal programs named for every letter of the alphabet, and all our problems went away.

Except it didn't quite happen like that in Orange County. You see, in Orange County, people weren't worried about apples—they had oranges. And as long as the citrus industry was healthy, so was our economy. The year 1929, in fact, was a big one for citrus—one of the biggest crops ever. The year 1930 saw a smaller harvest but higher prices. Local growers made $30 million on citrus in 1929, more than $40 million in 1930 and just over $35 million in 1931.

It was only then that things crashed. Returns dropped almost by half in 1932 and stayed under $20 million a year for the rest of the decade. It wasn't until 1942 that sales returned to their 1930 levels. In the meantime, prices were so low that some growers would dump part of their crop rather than try and sell it—drawing outrage in a time when hunger and malnutrition were serious problems.

Of course, Orange County also had the oil industry, pumping away in places like Brea and Huntington Beach. But despite the best efforts of County Assessor Jim Sleeper (the historian's grandfather), most of those profits still left the county, and the oil companies began cutting back on local employment.

This shanty was one of several in a homeless camp along the Santiago Creek, between Orange and Santa Ana, 1934. *Courtesy Jim Sleeper.*

Still, the unemployment rate here ran well below the national average, which got up around 25 percent at times. From 1933 to 1935, unemployment in Orange Country was between 9 and 15 percent, depending on the time of year and what crops were being harvested. But we also had a fair amount of underemployment—that is, places that kept workers on but had to cut their hours.

To take an example from my own family, my great-grandmother was working as a grader at the Consolidated Orange Growers packing house in Orange in the early 1930s. When the 1932 season came along, the manager, Frank Collins, called together the folks who had worked the year before and explained that he just couldn't afford to hire them all back. But, he said, if all of them would agree to take a pay cut, he could keep them all on the payroll, and everybody would at least make something that summer. They talked it over and agreed that less was better than none, and Collins hired them all back.

To thank him, the female employees pieced a quilt for Mr. Collins, embroidering their signature on each square they made. My great-grandmother's name is one of them. The Collins family still has the quilt to this day.

But labor relations were not always so cordial. In 1933 and again in 1938, Mexican farmworkers went on strike against Japanese vegetable and berry farmers in the western part of the county. The biggest strike was in 1936, when hundreds of Mexican orange pickers and packing house workers walked out during the height of the Valencia season. Tensions ran high over the next few weeks as worker meetings were broken up by armed men and replacement workers were attacked by strikers. In the end, the workers received a slight increase in pay and some improvements in working conditions, but their biggest goal—union recognition—went unfulfilled, and the strike soured relations between citrus growers and their Mexican workforce for years to come.

Homelessness was another problem here. There were "hobo camps" (as they were called in those days) scattered all across the county. There were several of them along Santiago Creek and the Santa Ana River—little shantytowns scattered among the undergrowth.

Things were really getting bad by 1932. Most of the local bank failures happened that year. The First National Bank of Newport Beach and Bank of Balboa both closed on the same day in February 1932. By 1935, a number of towns were without a bank, including Seal Beach, Yorba Linda, Cypress and San Juan Capistrano; Yorba Linda didn't have a bank again until 1945. In all, we lost about fifteen banks in Orange County, although some of them were later taken over by larger institutions, notably the Bank of America.

The local banks that did survive remained committed to their communities in a way the bigger banks never would be. At the First National Bank of Orange, the board of directors was determined not foreclose on anyone if it could at all avoid it. When people's credit was exhausted, the president, state Senator Nelson Edwards, would sometimes offer them personal loans out of his own pocket to help them keep going.

That's how all the early relief efforts were handled here—local institutions and local individuals tried their best to help people out. Churches, civic organizations—and not just the charitable organizations—all tried to do their part.

One thing that was popular here were cooperative organizations, where people could trade work for food and clothing. There were about twenty of them here in Orange County. People might have a little plot of farmland or would glean the fields. The women would make preserves or bake bread. They gathered clothes and castoffs and mended them. Several of the co-ops had their own stores, where people could pay by cash or trade. In Anaheim, they tried issuing local scrip. In Midway City, there was a co-op dairy. There were also soup kitchens and commodities stores, where food was available to anyone.

Camp Trabuco was the main Civilian Conservation Corps (CCC) camp in the Santa Ana Mountains in the 1930s. Located on the present site of Trabuco Elementary School, the men stationed there worked on mountain roads and flood control projects and were also pressed into service as firefighters. *Courtesy the Orange County Archives.*

Under President Hoover, cities and counties could borrow money for local projects. With the coming of President Roosevelt and the New Deal, the federal government started making actual grants for relief projects. Still, it was not until 1947 that Orange County was able to pay off the last of its Depression-era debt.

The State Emergency Relief Administration (and later the Works Progress Administration) handled most of the projects in Orange County. Between 1935 and 1937, the WPA spent more than $3 million on construction projects here, including schools, libraries, city halls, police stations, post offices, street improvements and storm drains.

The WPA also sponsored a historical research project for Orange County and local archaeological digs. Then there were preschools, sewing projects, library volunteers and all sorts of jobs for men and women. In 1939, the WPA had more than 2,300 employees on the payroll here.

The county also had four Civilian Conservation Corps (CCC) camps here in San Clemente, Trabuco Canyon, San Juan Hot Springs and Modjeska Canyon. The men stationed there did work in the national forest and on other local projects. There was also a state "transient worker" camp in the Santa Ana Canyon. All of them offered government-funded jobs for the unemployed.

In 1934, the Orange County Relief Administration was established to coordinate all the various efforts between the cities, the county, the state and the federal government. The Relief Administration also served as a job placement service for the WPA and other government agencies.

Between 1934 and 1936, there was about $7 million in federal, state and local relief funding distributed here. These relief funds didn't just go to the unemployed—in fact, in the mid-1930s, less than half of those receiving funds here were unemployed. Social Security was introduced in 1935, and by 1938, about 70 percent of our relief funds were going to seniors.

There were other ideas that came from outside the federal government as well. In 1934, before Social Security, Dr. Francis E. Townsend of Long Beach proposed an old-age pension plan where the federal government would issue $200 per month in scrip for people over sixty. The only catch was that the scrip all had to be spent that same month. It was all going to be paid for with additional taxes on people under sixty. Townsend's plan actually grew into a political party that survived for many years and advocated for all sorts of new government benefits.

Then there were Thirty-Dollar Thursdays—the Ham and Eggs movement—basically a monthly government handout to the needy. California voters turned that plan down twice, in 1938 and '39, despite support from Governor Culbert Olson.

Governor Olson was a Democrat and not very popular in Orange County. The county had long been a Republican stronghold. But as the Depression deepened, people blamed President Hoover for not doing enough and turned against the Republican Party. In 1932, Orange County gave Franklin Roosevelt a bare majority but still sent Republican representatives to Sacramento.

By 1936, the Democrats had taken the lead in voter registration in Orange County for the first time and won every state and national race here except for Tom Kuchel, who went to represent Anaheim in the Assembly. The only Republican-majority towns left here were Orange, Yorba Linda and San Juan Capistrano.

But as FDR stepped up the New Deal, he lost support in Orange County. Orange County voted Republican for governor in 1938 and went for Wendell Wilkie in 1940, when we sent Republicans back to Sacramento and Washington.

People were worried about expansion of government and the concentration of power in Washington. But others argued that these programs were being paid for with our taxes, so it was in the county's best interest to try to get as much of it back as possible—despite the strings attached.

Local residents line up for commodities distribution day at the WPA warehouse on East Fourth Street in downtown Santa Ana, circa 1939. *Courtesy the Orange County Archives.*

Inside the WPA commodities warehouse in Santa Ana, showing bulk food and other items bagged for individual use. *Courtesy the Orange County Archives.*

The 1933 Grand Jury members commented on how all these new government regulations actually made the work of the county welfare office more difficult. But, they added, no eligible persons had been turned down for assistance. By 1939, about 95 percent of the county's welfare spending was controlled by federal and state law.

To add to the economic woes, the 1930s were also an era of terrible natural disasters for Orange County. In 1933, the "Long Beach Earthquake" destroyed scores of buildings and killed several people here. In 1937, a big freeze damaged crops and cost the county about 20 percent of its citrus income in an already down year. Then in March 1938 came one of our worst floods ever, with a large loss of life and heavy property damage. The Santa Ana River left its bed and flowed right through downtown Anaheim and out to sea. Much of Buena Park was underwater, and the Mexican American communities at Atwood and La Jolla suffered terrible losses. Again, agriculture was hit hard, with the floodwaters depositing silt in some places more than one foot deep on top of fields and orange groves. Finally, in September 1939, there was a hurricane (or *chubasco*, as most everyone called it at the time) that tore up the coast and damaged all the local piers.

Throughout the '30s, it was just one thing after another. And despite the best efforts of our local communities, the county, the state and the federal government, Orange County—like the rest of America—struggled with economic depression on into the 1940s. It was only the industrial expansion of World War II that finally put America back on its feet.

In trying to compare the 1930s with today, it's important to remember what a different place Orange County was back then. For example, the delinquent property tax rate rose sharply here in the 1930s. But much of that was for small, unimproved lots—including new tracts laid out by speculators in the 1920s and never built on or still unsold. So, while tens of thousands of parcels went delinquent in 1938–39, it represented only about 1 percent of Orange County's assessed value.

The more striking figure is Orange County's population. The county had more than doubled in size in the 1920s. But in the 1930s, it grew from 118,000 residents to just 130,000. In fact, a number of communities actually lost population during the decade, including Fullerton, Orange, Placentia and Tustin. Huntington Beach grew by just 48 people in ten years, Anaheim by 36.

Yet despite tough times, voters in Santa Ana, Anaheim and Fullerton still voted for the Metropolitan Water District bonds in 1931 to build the Colorado River aqueduct, and county voters approved a major flood control bond act and bonds for the dredging of Newport Harbor in 1933.

Earthquake damage in downtown Santa Ana in March 1933. Several people were killed in the collapse of buildings there. *Courtesy the First American Corporation.*

Mexican American refugees carry what they can from the flooded village of Atwood, south of Placentia, after the devastating floods of March 1938. *Courtesy Gordon Walker.*

However, the facts and figures can only tell us part of the story of the Great Depression. It's the stories that put a human face on it that really convey what those years were like. Charles Parkman Taft was a prominent horticulturalist and rancher who developed several new varieties of fruits, including the Taft avocado. By the 1930s, he was an old man, living alone on his ranch north of Orange. Old-timers remember him driving slowly into town in what must have been about the last electric car in Orange. You'd see him get out, one said, and pull a dining room chair or some other small piece of furniture out of the back of the car. He'd take it into a secondhand shop and come out a few minutes later empty-handed. Then he would go into one of the markets and come out with a little bag of groceries, get in his car and drive slowly back to his lonely home. That's how he lived his last days, selling off his household goods one by one. He died in 1934.

The Great Depression changed the United States forever. New social programs, the expansion of the federal government and changes in labor relations all continue to affect us to this day.

# BREAKING NEW GROUND

## The Early Years of Knott's Berry Farm

Long before thrill rides and Halloween Haunts, long before Independence Hall and Camp Snoopy, even before Ghost Town and the Chicken Dinner Restaurant, Knott's Berry Farm was an actual berry farm. The story of the transformation of a roadside fruit stand into an internationally known tourist attraction is a long one. In the early years, the little farm grew largely out of necessity, as well as the boundless energy of Walter Knott.

Walter Knott was born in San Bernardino in 1889. His father, Reverend Elgin Knott, was a Methodist minister who owned an orange grove in Lordsburg (now La Verne). Walter's mother, Margaret Virginia (Dougherty) Knott (1866–1954), came from pioneer stock. She had come to California in 1868 in a covered wagon over the Southern Emigrant Trail.

But young Walter's life was turned upside down when his father passed away in 1896. Times were hard for Mrs. Knott, six-year-old Walter and his four-year-old brother, Elgin. The orange grove was sold, and the family moved to Pomona shortly before 1900.

Even as a boy, Walter Knott knew what he wanted to be when he grew up: a farmer. By the time he was ten years old, Walter was renting vacant lots around the neighborhood to grow vegetables that he sold from door to door. A few years later, at Pomona High School, he met the other great love of his life: Cordelia Hornaday (1890–1974).

In 1908, after just two years of high school, Walter set off for the Imperial Valley to find work in the rich farmlands there. A year later,

Walter Knott poses with rows of blackberries, circa 1924. It would be another decade before he introduced the Boysenberry to the world. *Courtesy the Orange County Archives.*

he and a cousin leased twenty acres in the Coachella Valley to grow vegetables. Through the dint of hard work, Walter made the farm pay.

Back in Pomona in 1910, Walter took a job with a local contractor. He was supposed to keep the books (he was "the poorest bookkeeper in the world," he would say in later years) but ended up as a construction foreman. It paid well. Walter built a house in Pomona (which still stands at 1040 West Fourth Street), and in 1911, he and Cordelia were married. Two years later, they welcomed their first child, Virginia.

## A DESERT HOMESTEAD

But Walter Knott was restless. Looking for new opportunities, in 1914 he moved his young family to a homestead near Newberry Springs, out on the Mojave Desert. Farming proved almost impossible in the dry desert valley, so while Cordelia stayed behind in their little adobe home to look after their growing family—son Russell, born in 1916, and daughter Rachel (Toni), born a year later—Walter was forced to find other work.

In 1916, he took a job at the famous old desert mining town of Calico, where a group of promoters hoped to work through the old tailings and extract the remaining silver. Then, in 1917, he managed to get on with a county road crew, building a new highway across the desert that would eventually become Route 66. It took three and a half years of struggle before Walter could prove up his homestead and receive 160 acres from the government. He owned that land for the rest of his life.

Still itching to be a farmer, Walter turned down a chance to return to his old contracting job in Pomona. Instead, he started off on a new venture. One of his cousins sometimes bought cattle from the Sacramento Ranch, near the little town of Shandon in northern San Luis Obispo County. The owners were looking for someone to grow crops on the ranch to feed the ranch hands. They'd provide the land if someone would do the farming. So Walter Knott became a tenant farmer.

The land was not considered all that productive, but Walter went to work and soon was not only feeding all the ranch hands but also had excess crops to sell in town. Cordelia also supplemented the family income by making and selling homemade candy. After three years of hard work, they had $2,500 in the bank. The children were getting older by then, so Walter started looking for a new opportunity near a bigger town with better schools.

Once again, it was a cousin who pointed the way. Jim Preston (1874–1958) was the son of one of his mother's older sisters. As a boy, Walter had sometimes worked for him on his ranch in Glendora. Now Preston proposed a partnership—the two of them would grow berries together at a place called Buena Park.

## Preston & Knott

Preston & Knott leased twenty acres along Grand Avenue. In December 1920, the Knotts left Shandon and moved to Buena Park. The Knott's youngest daughter, Marion, joined the family there in 1922.

While Jim Preston was the senior partner, it seems clear that it was Walter Knott who was the one on the ground, doing the work and driving the operation.

Like something out of *American Gothic*, Russell and Virginia Knott stand in the berry fields on their father's farm, circa 1923. *Courtesy the Orange County Archives.*

In fact, it's unclear if Preston even moved down from Glendora, although his son, J. Carson Preston, moved down to Buena Park in about 1926.

Preston & Knott's first year saw damaging frosts. Then, in 1922, prices dropped as the country slipped into an agricultural depression after World War I. Looking for ways to bring in more money, around 1923 Walter Knott decided to start selling berries direct to the public from a little roadside stand. This was not the famous "original" berry stand, which was not built until about 1924. It was "a lean-to sheltered with palm fronds," with a cigar box for a cash register. Preston & Knott also started a catalogue business, selling rootstock to other growers.

The Advance Blackberry was Preston & Knott's first big variety. It ripened by mid-April, up to three weeks before most other varieties. By 1924, the business had nineteen acres in Advance Blackberries, along with three acres of red raspberries, three acres of strawberries, three acres of dewberries, two acres of Loganberries and two acres of Macatawa blackberries—thirty-five acres in all.

But Walter was driven to keep looking for new ideas—and new berries. His next big find was the Youngberry. By 1927, Preston & Knott was pushing them hard, selling both fruit and rootstock throughout Southern California, Arizona and New Mexico. Besides berries, Preston & Knott also planted other crops, including asparagus and Cherry rhubarb.

## KNOTT'S BERRY PLACE

The year 1927 also marked the end of their lease in Buena Park, and Jim Preston and Walter Knott decided to break up their partnership. Preston moved to Norwalk and started his own berry ranch. But Knott was determined to stay in Buena Park. He approached his landlord with a proposition. Knott later recalled:

> By then, I knew what could be done with berries. Others were selling out or pulling up the bushes to drill for oil. No one else was in the field in a really big way, and we were coming up. It was wide open. I offered our landlord fifteen hundred dollars an acre for the ten. "It isn't worth fifteen hundred an acre, and you know it," he said. I said, "But I'll give you fifteen hundred an acre anyway." Then I sprang the catch. "I can't pay anything down,"

Knott's Berry Place, circa 1935. This was the first permanent building on the farm, built in 1928. Cordelia Knott's tea room is on the right. This building still stands along Grand Avenue (with a second story added) and now houses the Berry Market. *Courtesy the Orange County Archives.*

Harvesting Youngberries at Knott's Berry Place, circa 1933. This was Knott's big berry before the Boysenberry came along. *Courtesy the Orange County Archives.*

*I told him, "because we need our money to operate on and to put up a pie-and-coffee room and a larger berry market."*

*"Well, with nothing down," he said, "it is worth fifteen hundred an acre."*

That was a lot of money, but prices had been driven up by Orange County's oil boom of the 1920s. Even the interest on the land would be more than Preston & Knott had been paying in rent. But Walter was determined to own his own farm.

Ready to expand, during the winter of 1927–28, Walter built a new sales building along Grand Avenue, with a home for his family out back. The eighty-foot stucco structure included a nursery on the south end, a berry market in the middle and a "tea room" on the north, with seating for twenty.

The tea room was where Cordelia could sell sandwiches, fresh-baked rolls and jam, berry pie and ice cream during the harvest season. The place was designed so their home kitchen also opened up into the tea room. All of the Knott children were expected to do their share; the girls helped their mother in the tea room, and Russell worked for his father in the berry business. But in return, all of them were paid for their work.

In 1928, Knott's Berry Place opened for business (it would not become Knott's Berry Farm until the 1940s). About that same time, Walter decided to branch out. In the mid-1920s, he had purchased some land in Norco, out in Riverside County. There he built the Knott Nursery, adding a second retail outlet for his crops.

But the increasing weight of the Depression seems to have forced Walter to give up the Norco stand after just a few years. Crop prices were down, sales were off and land prices plummeted. The land he had promised to buy for $1,500 per acre was now worth $300 per acre at best. Friends suggested that he should back out of the deal and start over someplace else. But Walter would have none of it. He'd made his deal, and he was going to stand by it.

Walter even expanded his operation, renting adjoining acreage and buying more land. And even when the Depression was at its worst in the early 1930s, he still found the money to pay an advertising agency to keep promoting Knott's Berry Place and was buying ads in newspapers, magazines and on the radio.

# Mr. Boysen's Berry

All through the late '20s and early '30s, Walter Knott had been on the lookout for the next big berry, importing new rootstock from around the world to give it a try. Then, in 1932, George Darrow of the U.S. Department of Agriculture came to see Walter Knott. Back in the late 1920s, Douglas Coolidge, a Pasadena nurseryman, had told Darrow about a wonderful new berry, developed by a man by the name of Boysen. Now Coolidge was dead, and all Darrow knew was that Boysen was supposed to living somewhere in Southern California. He figured that an experienced berry grower like Walter Knott would know where to find him.

But Walter had never heard of a berry grower named Boysen. He checked the county directory, but the only Boysen he could find was Rudy Boysen, the park superintendent over in Anaheim. So Knott and Darrow went to see him.

Yes, Boysen said, he had developed a new berry variety—it was a cross between a blackberry, a Loganberry and a red raspberry. They were huge (by berry standards) and juicy, and they shipped well. Coolidge had even tried to market them back in about 1927 as the "Sensation Berry of the 20th Century." But then Coolidge died and Boysen broke his back in an accident, and that was the end of that. The last he'd seen of the berry, there were some growing on his in-laws' orange grove north of town, but the family had long since sold the property.

Inside the Berry Market, circa 1940 (part of the 1928 Knott's Berry Place building). Walter Knott is on the left. *Courtesy the Orange County Archives.*

"Would you take us there?" Walter asked. Boysen agreed, and amazingly, down in the weeds by an irrigation ditch, "two or three...rather scraggly" plants survived. There was no fruit on them at that time of year, but Walter decided to give them a try. With the permission of the new owners, he returned to get some cuttings, and in 1933, he had his first small crop of what he called the Boysenberry.

In 1934, with just one hundred vines, Knott's Berry Place produced 2,200 baskets of Boysenberries. They sold for twice the price of the old Youngberry, and it only took about half as many to fill a basket. By 1935, they had four acres in bearing and were ready to start selling rootstock to other growers. The Boysenberry was on its way.

# FRIED CHICKEN

Meanwhile, the Depression was dragging on, and money was still tight. To try and lure in more people, Cordelia decided to expand her tea room menu by offering a home-cooked fried chicken dinner.

Not that Cordelia wanted to run a restaurant. All the cooking was still done in her home kitchen, and her "Special Southern Chicken Dinner" was the only entrée on the menu. From the start, it came with salad, vegetable, cherry rhubarb, drinks and dessert. The price? Sixty-five cents. Not long after, ham was added for anyone who didn't want chicken.

But most everyone seemed to want chicken, and the little tea room began to grow—first to 40 seats and then out into a patio area with 30 more. In 1937, two new rooms were built and a real kitchen was added, bringing the total seating to 225.

At first, the tea room was only open during the berry season, but in 1937, the Knotts decided to try keeping it open all year round. During the harvest season that year, thousands of pounds of Boysenberries were frozen to guarantee pies all throughout the winter.

During the restaurant's first full year of operation in 1938, more than 265,000 chicken dinners were served. The chickens were purchased from dozens of local ranchers, all raised to Mrs. Knott's exacting standards. Cordelia had thirty-five people working for her in the kitchen, while her daughters managed a dining room staff of fifty-five. Virginia Knott also started a little gift shop in one corner. Two more dining rooms were added that year; now four hundred diners could be seated at one time.

Newspaper, radio and word-of-mouth advertising continued to spread the fame of Knott's Berry Place, urging folks to come out and visit.

# A ROADSIDE ATTRACTION

As the crowds grew and the lines stretched down the street, the Knotts started looking for ways to keep their guests occupied during the long wait.

Early in 1938, a rock garden was added on the west side of the building, with ferns and a waterfall powered by the pump from an old tractor. Colored lights, hidden in the plants, completed the scene. The many coins

A volcano was built alongside the Chicken Dinner Restaurant in 1939 to hide a concrete standpipe that was part of the farm's irrigation system. A little red devil in the box in the foreground turned a crank that set it smoking and rumbling. *Courtesy the Orange County Archives.*

tossed into the water were donated to Mission San Juan Capistrano to help with its restoration.

Next to the rock garden, Russell Knott set up a display of fluorescent minerals he had collected on his many trips to the desert. Visitors could turn on a black light that made the colors leap out. In another room, a collection of antique music boxes was on display.

In 1939, the restaurant was expanded yet again, including a new wing on the west side of the building. That presented a problem. Knott later recalled:

> *There was a real eyesore right outside the new room's windows—an unsightly stand pipe that stood some ten or twelve feet high. Now, we had to irrigate our fields, and the stand pipe was a very necessary part of our irrigation system, so there was no way we could eliminate it. We just had to figure out a way to make it look more attractive. I spent several days*

*analyzing the problem, trying to think of every possible solution. Then I just stopped thinking about it. One morning while I was shaving, the answer came to me: we'll make a volcano out of it and put a desert cactus garden all around it!*

Built of eighteen tons of volcanic rock hauled in from Pisgah Mountain out on the Mojave Desert, the volcano featured a boiler to create steam and a rumbling noise machine. They planted some Joshua trees and cactus all around, and there was even a little red devil who turned the crank to make it go.

By 1941, the displays had grown to include more music boxes, a two-hundred-year-old grandfather clock, an old millstone, a huge slab of redwood, a hive of honeybees, a Mexican carreta, an old stagecoach said to have been robbed by Black Bart and a replica of one of George Washington's fireplaces at Mount Vernon. (The fireplace and the millstone are still on display today.)

Knott's Berry Place had become a roadside attraction.

## GHOST TOWN VILLAGE

All of these early exhibits would pale next to Walter Knott's next idea. He had always been fascinated with the pioneer days of the Old West. He had grown up on the stories of his Grandmother Dougherty, who had crossed the desert by covered wagon in 1868. Now he wanted to tell that story to a new generation of Americans.

In 1915, at the Panama-Pacific International Exhibition in San Francisco, Walter and Cordelia had seen a cyclorama—a curved painting, with scenery and props built in front of it and special lighting to give it a realistic, three-dimensional effect. Why not tell the story of the pioneers that same way? But the idea kept growing. Why not a western building to house the painting? In fact, why not an entire western ghost town, re-created at Knott's Berry Place?

Work on Knott's "Ghost Town Village" (as it was originally known) began in 1940. At first, Walter thought that it might take six months or perhaps a year to build. In fact, he went on building for nearly two decades. He wanted Ghost Town to be both entertaining and educational.

About the same time the Ghost Town idea was coming together, a young artist named Paul Swartz arrived on the farm hoping to make a little money cutting silhouettes for the waiting crowds. He caught Walter's enthusiasm for Ghost Town and soon joined in on its design and construction.

Knott sent men out who "drove through California for months, buying up old barns, buggies, tools, furniture, door and window frames—everything they could find that might fit into Ghost Town." Swartz did research and designed the buildings around the salvaged materials. As Walter Knott explained in 1942:

> Every time I have the opportunity to get away for a couple of days I like to visit the ghost towns of the west for we are continually seeking materials with which to reconstruct the ghost town here at Knott's Berry Place. By securing a building here, part of another there, an old bar in one place or something else somewhere else we add to the picture we are attempting to portray—a composite picture of the ghost towns of the west as they appeared in '49 and the early '50s. We are not collecting museum pieces nor is it the intention to build a museum. Our thought is to collect a town but as that is impossible we try to do the next best thing—build or reconstruct a ghost town that will be authentic and show life as it was lived in the early days.

The biggest building was the two-story hotel, variously known as the Gold Trails or the Old Trails Hotel. Originally built in 1868 in a mining town near Prescott, Arizona, it was disassembled and the parts used to build a home for the cyclorama.

As the buildings rose, woodcarver Andy Anderson populated them with hand-carved wooden figures posed in various scenes—a Chinese laundry, an assay office, a sheriff's office—but from the start, the best-known figure was "Sad Eye Joe," the lone resident of the Ghost Town jail. He startled visitors by not only speaking to them but also knowing their names and little tidbits about them. That part of Ghost Town remains unchanged to this day.

At the same time Ghost Town was under construction, two adobe buildings were constructed from bricks made right there on the farm. The first was a studio for another artist who had gotten caught up in Walter's schemes, Paul von Klieben. The other adobe was the "Little Chapel by the Lake" (now gone), built to house one of Von Klieben's most unusual paintings: a portrait of Jesus Christ painted with special fluorescent paints so that when black lights were switched on, Christ's eyes seem to open and look directly at the

The Ghost Town Grill under construction, circa 1941, showing how older materials were reused to create an authentic Old West feel. *Courtesy the Orange County Archives.*

viewer. Von Klieben called it *The Transfiguration*. It opened to the public on December 11, 1941.

Paul von Klieben soon replaced Paul Swartz as the "art director" for Ghost Town, and Walter Knott was always proud to sing his praises. "I attribute much of the success of Ghost Town to this man," he said many times.

By mid-1941, Ghost Town was ready to open to the public. In July, Knott's began a big advertising push, not just in the newspapers but also in its own magazine, the *Ghost Town News*, edited by a former Los Angeles stockbroker, Nichols Field Wilson. The magazine was published until 1946 and featured stories of the Old West, some by well-known writers and historians.

But the cyclorama that started it all was slow in coming. Yet another artist, Fritz Zilling, had been hired to paint the curved canvas, but the work dragged on for months with no end in sight. Finally, Paul von Klieben stepped in to finish the job, adding the foreground and a fluorescent night scene. In just a few short weeks, the twenty- by fifty-foot painting was complete.

On Washington's Birthday, February 22, 1942, the "Covered Wagon Show" opened to the public for the first time. Like all of Ghost Town, the prerecorded, three-minute presentation was free to the public.

Knott's Berry Place had gone from farm to roadside attraction to theme park.

# THE MAN BEHIND IT ALL

While the entire Knott family contributed to the success of Knott's Berry Farm, there seems little doubt that it never would have happened without Walter Knott. He was a man who wasn't afraid of hard work and was willing to sacrifice to get the job done. He was focused—almost driven—as he pushed forward to reach his goals.

Yet he was also imaginative, inventive and always willing to try something new. The things that worked, he kept; the things that didn't, he dropped. He understood the value of publicity, the need to understand what your customers wanted and the importance of setting goals. During his early years, he learned how to make the most of a bad situation and how to grow in response to outside challenges and opportunities.

Looking back, he always seemed to be able to find the bright side in tough times. Take the Depression, for example. "We started out to have the best berry farm, and perhaps the biggest berry farm in California," he recalled in 1972, "and no intention of getting into all this other business, but goals change as you go along and the depression was a blessing in disguise in that it got us into other things besides just the berry farming, and we've enjoyed the other things and the building of Ghost Town and saving these historic relics very much, and I have to thank the depression for it."

Walter Knott always credited Cordelia for her part as well. "My wife has always been a hard working but cautious and practical woman," he said in later years, "and as such, she acts as a good balance for me. I'm a bit optimistic and impulsive. If a man has a tendency to charge ahead too fast, it does him a whale of a lot of good to have to sell his ideas to his partner and convince her that he can pay for them. I did a better job of outlining and considering my position when I knew I'd have to justify it with my wife. Cordelia and I have always worked as a team; I apply the gas and she applies the brake."

Cordelia Knott died in 1974. Walter Knott died in 1981, just short of his ninety-second birthday. Their children and grandchildren continued to run Knott's Berry Farm until it was sold in 1997. It remains one of America's most popular theme parks.

# BOUNDARY BATTLES
# OF THE POSTWAR BOOM

The 1950s and '60s were a time of unprecedented growth in Orange County, with the population soaring from 216,000 in 1950 to more than 1 million by 1963. But the era was not without its conflicts. A dozen new cities were born during that time, and the existing cities spread out through annexation. It was perhaps inevitable that there would be squabbles and boundary disputes as cities old and new tried to position themselves for future growth.

The boom followed the end of World War II, beginning in Los Angeles and spreading out from there. Thousands of young servicemen and women had passed through Southern California during the war. Now many of them decided to return, settle down and start families here. Before long, they were joined by their parents, grandparents, aunts, uncles, cousins and a surge of baby boomer children.

In Orange County, the boom really took off around 1950. That year, 5,500 residential building permits were issued in the county. Five years later, that number had reached nearly 26,000. The total peaked again in 1962, with 33,200 permits issued.

The growth was especially rapid in the flat farmlands on the western side of the county. Besides being closer to Los Angeles, the largely level terrain made things easier for homebuilders, and much of the area was planted to row crops rather than citrus, making it easy for farmers to simply not plant one year so the developers could plant houses instead. Garden Grove, for example, swelled from 3,700 residents in 1950 to 45,000 by 1956, making it one of the faster-growing communities in America.

Cities both old and new were rushing to annex as much territory as they could. And by law, those annexations had to be contiguous—that is, one city cannot cross another. Some of these incorporations and annexations were defensive, designed to block a neighboring city from moving into an area. Others were proactive, seeking to protect existing communities and their way of life. Sometimes they followed existing boundary lines, such as school districts. Sometimes they were based on a single large property owner wanting to be in (or out) of a particular city.

A glance at a modern map of Orange County shows the remnants of many of these old boundary battles. Notice how Stanton extends along Beach Boulevard south to Garden Grove Boulevard, with more Garden Grove to the west, connected by only a tiny shoestring. Or the long tail of Garden Grove along the east side of Ward Street, almost to Mile Square Park, dividing Santa Ana from Westminster.

Buena Park has its own tail, south along Holder Avenue, dividing Cypress from Garden Grove. And then there's little La Palma, wedged in by Buena Park along the county line. Or look at Anaheim's jagged southern boundary or the long journey up the Santa Ana Canyon into Anaheim Hills. Or how Orange surrounds Villa Park. Then there are the various "islands" of unincorporated territory still scattered throughout the county. Each of these boundaries is a story.

Santa Ana was a pioneer in this sort of aggressive annexation. In the 1920s, it tried to annex much of area west of Orange. When local voters turned it down at the polls, it took its revenge by annexing just enough land to build Santa Ana Boulevard in an attempt to lure traffic away from Orange.

To the south, Santa Ana also dreamed of extending itself all the way to the coast. In 1928, it tried to annex six thousand acres in South Santa Ana and Costa Mesa, but after a "bitter campaign," local residents voted it down five to one. But the battles of the 1920s were mere skirmishes compared to the hectic days of the 1950s and '60s.

*Opposite, top*: Supporters of Costa Mesa's failed 1947 incorporation attempt present their case to the Orange County Board of Supervisors. The city finally incorporated in 1953. *Courtesy the Old Orange County Courthouse Museum.*

*Opposite, bottom*: Posting new street signs was just one of many jobs that kept county employees busy when Garden Grove began to grow in the early 1950s. Later, the city would take over those duties. *Courtesy the Old Orange County Courthouse Museum.*

# THE WESTERN FRONT

Buena Park was the first of our new postwar cities. It felt threatened by expansion from Anaheim and Fullerton and voted to incorporate in January 1953. Thanks to annexations, the new city tripled in size within two years.

Garden Grove was close on its heels. In 1954, it proposed a twenty-three-square-mile city, north to Anaheim, east to the Santa Ana River and far enough south and west to even make Westminster a little nervous. Complaints poured in from folks north of Katella Avenue, as well as out west in the little community of Sun Gardens near Newland and Garden Grove Boulevard.

In the days before the Local Agency Formation Commission (LAFCO, formed in 1965), the board of supervisors not only authorized incorporation elections but also set the boundaries for new cities after hearing arguments from property owners on all sides. It reduced the proposed city of Garden Grove to just nine square miles and set the election for May 10, 1955. The measure failed by just a few hundred votes.

A new, twelve-square-mile proposal soon followed, running more to the east and west. It included Sun Gardens, which had come around on the idea of incorporation. Much of the opposition came from the local farmers. Others argued that the town already had everything it needed through a series of special assessment districts that funded sewers, streetlights and even downtown parking. The county could continue to take care of the rest, they said.

But as rapid growth continued to bring more and more suburban residents to the area, the tide turned, and a second election in April 1956 passed easily, 5,780 to 2,346. The new city of Garden Grove immediately began looking to annex more territory to the south and west.

That kicked up the pressure on Stanton, where incorporation petitions had been circulating for some time. Like Garden Grove, it had initially proposed a much larger city (six square miles), only to see the board of supervisors cut it to just one square mile. But at least it was a start, and on May 15, 1956 (just a month after Garden Grove), the residents voted 185 to 126 to incorporate.

Thanks to annexations and continued development, by 1960 the city of Stanton had tripled in size, and the population had grown from about 1,300 to more than 12,000.

Next to incorporate was Westminster. The original plan was to include two adjoining 1920s subdivisions—Midway City and Barber City—under the temporary name of Tri-City. Midway City later backed out of the

Part of the audience at an incorporation hearing before the Orange County Board of Supervisors for the proposed city of Garden Grove, circa 1955. There was heated debate on both sides. *Author's collection.*

Main Street and Garden Grove Boulevard in downtown Garden Grove in 1956, the year the city finally incorporated. *Courtesy the Old Orange County Courthouse Museum.*

Tract housing going up in the new city of Stanton, 1956. A single tract might include one hundred to two hundred homes. *Courtesy the Orange County Archives.*

deal, but Westminster and Barber City went ahead on March 31, 1957, and incorporated as the city of Tri-City by a bare majority of 1,096 to 1,008. In a second election, five months later, the city was officially renamed Westminster. Parts of Midway City remain unincorporated county territory to this day.

Fountain Valley incorporated later that same year to protect itself from Santa Ana. The population was still small in 1957 (only 154 votes were cast in the incorporation election), but the area soon began to grow as tract housing replaced farmland. A master plan was adopted in 1961 calling for a mix of residential and commercial development.

## COW TOWNS

Buena Park's active annexation program spurred ranchers south and west of the new city to think about incorporation. The area was almost entirely rural, with dairies and poultry ranches dominating. Dairy farming ran second only to Valencia oranges here in the mid-1950s as our largest cash

Dairy cows were still a common sight in the Cypress area in 1969, but increasing development would eventually drive them all away. *Courtesy the Orange County Archives.*

crop, with poultry coming in third. Ironically, many of these dairy farmers had only arrived a few years before, when they had been pushed out of Los Angeles County by increasing residential development.

In the area below Buena Park, west of Miller Street and south to La Palma Avenue, there were more cows than people, and the ranchers wanted it to stay that way. So they hit on a novel plan. If the area would incorporate as a city, they could simply refuse to create any residential zoning and keep the area rural.

In 1955—with Buena Park threatening to annex about half the area and new subdivisions closing in—the ranchers petitioned the board of supervisors to hold an incorporation election. Taking their cue from the new theme park about to open nearby, they dubbed their new city Dairyland. There were just ninety-two registered voters in the area, and seventy-four of them went to the polls on October 11, 1955, to vote fifty-five to nineteen for cityhood.

The new city of Dairyland had no retail shops or businesses, and the first city hall was an office in a hay barn. The city hired a city manager, a city engineer and a police chief and contracted with the county for most everything else.

Looking along Lincoln Avenue at Walker Street in downtown Cypress, circa 1941. The little town was not originally included in the new Dairy City but was soon annexed, name and all. *Courtesy the Orange County Archives.*

The new idea proved popular, and within a year, two other "cow towns" had incorporated—Dairy Valley in Los Angeles County (now the city of Cerritos) and Dairy City. But there was a flaw in their plan. Because it had never even been a town before, the new city of Dairyland was divided between five different school districts—Centralia, Buena Park and Cypress Elementary School Districts and the Anaheim and Fullerton Union High School Districts. And the same lack of residential zoning that protected the dairies and ranches kept property values low, prompting the various districts to start condemning the cheaper land by eminent domain for school sites. By 1963—when only about fifty Dairyland youngsters attended public schools—there were already three schools in the city, with three more planned. By 1965, 10 percent of the tiny city had been taken off the tax rolls by schools.

In 1964, the city fathers finally faced the inevitable and drew up a new zoning map opening up more than 70 percent of the community for residential development. In February 1965, local voters approved bonds to build a modern water and sewer system. To make a clean break, they also voted to rename Dairyland after the major arterial street in the area. And so the city of La Palma was born.

The dairy farmers south of Dairyland were stirred to action when it was proposed to incorporate Los Alamitos, Cypress and Stanton as a single city. Instead, they decided to incorporate on their own as Dairy City.

Like Dairyland, Dairy City was not really a town at that point, with residents in the proposed city getting their mail from Cypress, Buena Park, Westminster, Anaheim, Stanton, Los Alamitos and even Artesia, over the line in L.A. County. But on June 26, 1956, they came together to vote 217 to 73 to become their own city. "We didn't want to incorporate but we were forced into cityhood as a means of preserving our way of life," Mayor Jake Van Dyke told the papers. Two of the council candidates tied and agreed to flip a coin to decide the winner, with Jacob Van Leeuwen winning the toss and Martin Olstenhoorn appointed city clerk as a consolation prize.

At the same election, a straw vote was taken on permanent name for the new city. Voters were asked to decide between Dairy City, Los Coyotes, Lincoln City (for Lincoln Avenue) or Cypress. Cypress was the preferred choice, followed by Lincoln City, with Dairy City running a distant fourth—this despite the fact that Dairy City did not then include the nearby town of Cypress. But Dairy City it was until another election could be held to change the name.

In the meantime, Dairy City annexed downtown Cypress along Walker Street, north of Lincoln Avenue (most of the businesses along Lincoln had recently been lost to street widening). A month later, in August 1957, voters officially renamed their city Cypress.

From the start, the City of Cypress welcomed industrial development (there was already a major oil tank farm there), but like Dairyland, it refused to establish any residential zoning. The two cities also shared the same city manager, Burt Wesenberg, and a combined police force, with Cypress paying about two-thirds of Wesenberg's salary.

When a new majority on the city council decided to open up the community for residential development in 1960, they also voted to fire Wesenberg (who kept his Dairyland job, however). The joint staffing arrangement quickly fell apart, and the two cities went their own separate ways.

# INTO THE '60s

By 1960, it was obvious to everyone that Orange County's agricultural days were numbered. Not that there wasn't plenty of undeveloped land, but with the Santa Ana Freeway pushing its way through the county and an expanding supply of imported water available, even the big ranches in the South County knew that someday homes and businesses would replace crops and cattle.

As in the rest of the county, the few little towns in the south began to think about incorporation. San Juan Capistrano was the first, originally proposing to incorporate with Dana Point and Capistrano Beach as a single city. When that plan fell apart, Capistrano proposed extending its city limits all the way to the ocean, dividing Capistrano Beach and Dana Point. When those communities protested, Capistrano had to settle for a smaller city, which incorporated in 1961. It would be another twenty-seven years before Dana Point and Capistrano Beach voted to incorporate as the city of Dana Point.

New concerns were arising as well. Just as the dairy farmers had incorporated to try to protect their way of life, other county residents wanted to avoid the cookie-cutter, small-lot subdivisions that were swallowing up so much of Southern California. The citrus ranchers in the little community of Villa Park, for example, incorporated in 1962 and established a minimum twenty-thousand-square-foot "estate lot" requirement. The boundary lines for the new city had been carefully drawn to leave out many of the areas that opposed incorporation, giving Villa Park a jagged boundary with the adjoining city of Orange.

Of course, not all the owners of large tracts wanted to be in cities that restricted residential development (or any development, as in cow towns). Several large landowners east of Villa Park wanted to be in the city of Orange, and by 1965, Orange had completely surrounded its little neighbor.

Meanwhile, Orange was trying to come to terms with Anaheim, which had "jumped the river" and begun annexing its way up the south side of the Santa Ana Canyon a few years before. With Fullerton, Placentia and the new West County cities hemming them in, Anaheim really had no place else to go. As it moved up into what became known as Anaheim Hills, Orange negotiated an agreement to keep Anaheim from annexing south of the ridgeline. Orange needed those hills not for homes (they were not built until decades later) but for water tanks, to provide a gravity flow for the community.

Orange also plotted with Tustin to annex north and south to meet at Fairhaven, along Tustin Avenue, to create a barrier to the city of Santa Ana, which Tustin feared was heading for the foothills. "This idea of being big for bigness sake, as far as I'm concerned, is for the birds," Orange's first city manager, George Weimer, used to say.

Seniors wheel along a bike path in Laguna Hills Leisure World in this circa 1970 publicity photograph. *Courtesy the Orange County Archives.*

But the most audacious plan for these "shoestring" annexations came from developer Ross Cortese. He had already developed the suburban community of Rossmoor between 1956 and 1960 and then turned to seniors-only developments, opening Seal Beach Leisure World in 1961.

Then Cortese turned south and proposed a Laguna Hills Leisure World on 5,300 acres south of El Toro. Hoping to secure city services and a dependable water supply, in 1962 Cortese approached both the City of Laguna Beach and the new City of San Juan Capistrano about annexation. When they turned him down, he looked to Santa Ana, which quickly agreed to begin proceedings to annex a three-hundred-foot-wide strip (the legal minimum) eight and a half miles along the Santa Ana Freeway to take in the proposed senior community. The Irvine Company, the El Toro Marine Corps Air Station and even the proposed University of California–Irvine objected. Then the Irvine Company sued over the plan, and that was end of that.

Leisure World did get built, however, and in 1999 voted to incorporate as the city of Laguna Woods. But if Cortese had succeeded, there would be no city of Irvine as we know it today. His shoestring annexation would have cut the lower end of the ranch in two.

And it was the lower end of the ranch—the flat valley floor—that was ripe for development in the 1960s. The Irvine Company recognized that. Prompted in part by the search for a new campus for the University of California, in 1960 the company commissioned a development study for the entire eighty-eight-thousand-acre ranch. First to be developed would be the area around the university. Then other areas would be developed as a series of suburban "villages." Agriculture, the company realized, would continue for many years, while industry, retail and office development slowly replaced cows, citrus and lima beans.

Incorporation was expected to be years away, but as the company tired of dealing with county planners, and adjoining cities began looking at annexations on the ranch, it joined with local residents in 1971 to support cityhood. The election on December 21, 1971, passed 3,224 to 1,515, and the city of Irvine was born.

The last of the 1960s incorporations in Orange County was the city of Yorba Linda, after more than a decade of struggle. As usual, local residents were first spurred to action by the approach of other cities. Incorporation talk began in 1957 but could not find enough support. It was revived in 1961, when there was also talk of merging with the city of Placentia. But neither plan ever took off. Two years later, with Placentia closing in, incorporation supporters launched another petition drive and again fell short.

The problem was the oil and gas reserves in the surrounding hills. State law said that if owners of more than half of the local assessed valuation objected to incorporation, no election could be held. But the County of Orange also allowed out-of-town owners of oil and gas leases to count toward Yorba Linda's assessed value. The *Yorba Linda Star* lambasted the supervisors for their lack of concern about the local residents. A lawsuit was filed, but the board's decision held.

During 1965, while the matter was on appeal, local residents held meetings with Placentia, Brea and Anaheim to consider annexing to one of those cities. In the end, they decided not to join Anaheim but were taking a hard look at Placentia when the appellate court overturned the use of mineral rights for assessed value. Now it was the county's turn to appeal, but the California Supreme Court upheld the ruling.

At long last, Yorba Lindans could finally head to the polls, and on October 24, 1967, the community voted 1,963 to 638 to become a city. "Yorba Linda seemed to breathe a collective sigh of relief, that now the question was settled once and for all," librarian March Butz wrote in her 1970 history of the city.

By then, the mad rush to incorporate or annex had largely come to an end here. The surge of residential development had finally caught up with the huge increase in population, and the energy crisis and the runaway inflation of the 1970s finally slowed Orange County's phenomenal growth. Planned communities had also replaced the pell-mell development of the boom years. They faced other challenges in their push for approval and eventual incorporation, but boundary battles were usually not among them.

Today, most of the battles are over the few remaining "county islands"—unincorporated areas between cities. How much of the county will, or should, remain unincorporated is debated on all sides. But one thing is certain: even with thirty-four cities and a population topping 3 million, Orange County will continue to grow.

# SUGGESTED READING

Armor, Samuel, ed. *The History of Orange County, California with Biographical Sketches.* Los Angeles, CA: Historic Record Company, 1921.

Bollman, Ivana Freeman. *Westminster Colony, California, 1869–1879.* Santa Ana, CA: Friis-Pioneer Press, 1983.

Brigandi, Phil. *Orange County Place Names A to Z.* San Diego, CA: Sunbelt Publications, 2006.

Brown, Alan K., ed. *A Description of Distant Roads: Original Journals of the First Expedition into California, 1769–1770 by Juan Crespí.* San Diego, CA: San Diego State University Press, 2001.

Butz, March. *Yorba Linda, Its History.* 2nd ed. Covina, CA: Taylor Publishing Company, 1979.

Cleland, Robert Glass. *The Cattle on a Thousand Hills: Southern California, 1850–1880.* 2nd ed. San Marino, CA: Huntington Library, 1951.

Coleman, Fern Hill. "History of the Celery Industry." *Orange County History Series.* Vol. 3. Santa Ana, CA: Orange County Historical Society, 1939.

Cramer, Esther. *Brea: The City of Oil, Oranges and Opportunity.* Brea, CA: City of Brea, 1992.

Doig, Leroy. *The City of Garden Grove.* Santa Ana, CA: Friis-Pioneer Press, 1977.

Donaldson, Stephen E., and William A. Myers. *Rails through the Orange Groves: A Centennial Look at the Railroads of Orange County, California.* 2 vols. Glendale, CA: Trans-Anglo Books, 1989–90.

Friis, Leo J. *Orange County through Four Centuries.* Santa Ana, CA: Pioneer Press, 1965.

Gonzalez, Gilbert G. *Labor and Community: Mexican Citrus Worker Villages in a Southern California County, 1900–1950.* Urbana: University of Illinois Press, 1994.

Guinn, James M. "History of the Movements for the Division of Los Angeles County." *Annual Publication of the Historical Society of Southern California* (1888–89).

Hallan-Gibson, Pamela. *The Golden Promise: An Illustrated History of Orange County.* 2nd ed. Northridge, CA: Windsor Publications, 2002.

*Huntington Beach News.* "History of New Coast Road, Movement Started in Sunset Beach." October 8, 1926.

Lin, Patricia. "Perspectives on the Chinese in Nineteenth Century Orange County." *Journal of Orange County Studies*, nos. 3–4 (Fall 1989/Spring 1990).

MacIver, Ron, and Elfriede MacIver. *Images of America: La Palma.* Charleston, SC: Arcadia Publishing, 2008.

McCawley, William. *The First Angelinos: The Gabrielino Indians of Los Angeles County.* Banning and Novato, CA: A Malki Museum Press/Ballena Press Cooperative Publication, 1996.

Meadows, Don. *Historic Place Names in Orange County.* Balboa Island, CA: Paisano Press, 1966.

———. "The March of Portolá." In *The Historical Volume and Reference Works…Orange County.* Whittier, CA: Historical Publishers, 1963.

————. "The Original Site of Mission San Juan Capistrano." *Southern California Quarterly* (September 1967).

Merritt, Christopher, and Eric Lynxwiler. *Knott's Preserved: From Boysenberry to Theme Park, the History of Knott's Berry Farm.* Santa Monica, CA: Angel City Press, 2010.

Pritchard, Robert L. "Orange County During the Depressed Thirties: A Study in Twentieth-Century California Local History." *Southern California Quarterly* (June 1968).

Sleeper, Jim. *Jim Sleeper's Orange County Almanac of Historical Oddities.* 3 editions. Trabuco Canyon, CA: OCUSA Press, 1971–82.

————. "The Night They Burned Chinatown." *Orange County Illustrated* (June 1970).

————. *Turn the Rascals Out! The Life and Times of Orange County's Fighting Editor, Dan M. Baker.* Trabuco Canyon: California Classics, 1973.

*South Coast News.* "Highway History Story of Pioneers' Battle." January 20, 1933.

Stephenson, Terry. *Caminos Viejos: Tales Found in the History of California.* Santa Ana, CA: Press of the Santa Ana High School and Junior College, 1930.

Walker, Doris. *Dana Point Harbor/Capistrano Bay: Home Port for Romance.* 4th ed. Dana Point, CA: To-The-Point Press, 1995.

————. *Orange County: A Centennial Celebration.* Houston, TX: Pioneer Publications, 1989.

Warner, Jonathan. "The Anaheim Scrip Plan." *Southern California Quarterly* (Fall 2008).

[Wilson, Albert]. *History of Los Angeles County, California.* Oakland, CA: Thompson & West, 1880. Reprint, 1959.

# INDEX

# ABOUT THE AUTHOR

Phil Brigandi has been researching and writing local history since 1975 and is the author of nearly two dozen books and hundreds of articles on the history of Orange, Riverside and San Diego Counties. He has worked as a newspaper columnist, museum curator and research consultant, and from 2003 to 2008, he served as Orange County archivist. He has been active with many historical organizations, including the Orange Community Historical Society (joining the board of directors at age eighteen), the Orange County Historical Society, the Orange County Historical Commission, Los Compadres con Libros, the Los Angeles Corral of The Westerners and the Ancient and Honorable Order of E Clampus Vitus.

*Visit us at*
www.historypress.net

...............................................................

*This title is also available as an e-book*

# ABOUT THE AUTHOR

P hil Brigandi has been researching and writing local history since 1975 and is the author of nearly two dozen books and hundreds of articles on the history of Orange, Riverside and San Diego Counties. He has worked as a newspaper columnist, museum curator and research consultant, and from 2003 to 2008, he served as Orange County archivist. He has been active with many historical organizations, including the Orange Community Historical Society (joining the board of directors at age eighteen), the Orange County Historical Society, the Orange County Historical Commission, Los Compadres con Libros, the Los Angeles Corral of The Westerners and the Ancient and Honorable Order of E Clampus Vitus.